Following GOD'S CALL

D0166542

Following GOD'S CALL

Individual Volunteers in Mission

Nalt Whitehurst

Betty Whitehurst

Walter A. Whitehurst &
Betty C. Whitehurst

Abingdon Press/Nashville

FOLLOWING GOD'S CALL
INDIVIDUAL VOLUNTEERS IN MISSION

Library of Congress Cataloging-in-Publication Data

Whitehurst, Walter A.
  Following God's call : individual volunteers in mission / Walter A. and Betty C. Whitehurst.
    p. cm.
  ISBN 978-0-687-49109-4 (binding: pbk., adhesive perfect : alk. paper)
  1. United Methodist Volunteers in Mission. 2. Missionary stories. I. Whitehurst, Betty C. II. Title.

  BV2550.W45 2008
  266'.76--dc22

                                                                              2008016999

08 09 10 11 12 13 14 15 16 17—10 9 8 7 6 5 4 3 2 1

MANUFACTURED IN THE UNITED STATES OF AMERICA

We dedicate this book to its real authors—persons who have served as individual volunteers and who have written eloquently about their volunteer experiences.

We dedicate this book to our readers—persons who are interested in mission and who want to learn more about what it is like to be an individual volunteer.

We dedicate this book to the many persons throughout the world who welcome individual volunteers, make them feel at home in a strange new setting, and help them find ways to serve the Lord that benefit both the local people and the volunteers.

To God be the glory.

Contents

Acknowledgments

WE EXTEND OUR MOST HEARTFELT THANKS TO:

Our colleagues in the office of United Methodist Volunteers In Mission, Southeastern Jurisdiction, for their continuing support of the Individual Volunteer program and of our ministry and mission.

Our colleagues in the Mission Volunteers office of the General Board of Global Ministries of The United Methodist Church, for their encouragement.

Our daughter, Mónica Whitehurst, for her assistance with research, typing, and proofreading, and for her helpful suggestions.

To Our Readers

Dear friends: I am interested in serving as a short-term volunteer in mission. What are my opportunities? I am a former teacher, reading specialist, college professor, certified nurse's aide, cook, and whatever. I am in good health but kinda old.

— AN E-MAIL FROM A POTENTIAL VOLUNTEER

*E*very year, thousands of people volunteer to serve in mission around the world. We have had the privilege of knowing many of them in our work with the United Methodist Volunteers In Mission (UMVIM). Their stories have touched us deeply, and so we are writing this book to share some of those stories with you.

After a brief history of the individual volunteer movement and an introduction to the program, we will tell the volunteers' stories. You will enjoy getting to know the volunteers as you read about their experiences.

Without exception, the accounts in this book are true stories told to us by real volunteers, writing soon after the actual experiences. The volunteers who are named have given their permission; otherwise, the names have been omitted.

Who will benefit from reading the stories? Certainly persons who are considering the possibility of serving as individual volunteers in mission can learn a lot from reading about the experiences of those who have served.

Also, former individual volunteers may want to purchase and read this book. Their volunteer service has affected their own lives in important ways. They will enjoy the stories of other volunteers and identify with and understand what they read in this book.

One thought unanimously expressed by volunteers attending the individual volunteer orientation/training events is their joy at meeting others who have similar interests and who also feel called by God to serve as volunteers. They realize that they are not alone—they are part of a larger community.

Not only potential future volunteers and former volunteers but also laypersons who would like to learn about the global work of the church can find inspiration in the writings of individual volunteers who share their joys and hard times, their adjustment to other cultures, and their spiritual and emotional growth.

We Americans usually start off by asking how much something costs. Individual volunteers, by contrast, grasp the concept of acting on faith in God. They have learned that if a person is committed to serving in response to God's call, somehow the financial resources are provided. Indeed, one of the blessings of living in the United States of America is that we have the capability of raising funds for such service. In many countries, persons would like to volunteer but are not blessed with financial resources.

Pastors may find some good sermon illustrations from the experiences of individual volunteers recorded in this book. Whenever we have spoken in churches, we have shared many of these experiences, and members of those congregations have related well to these stories. Such personal testimonies challenge the listeners to imagine how they might better serve God by serving people, not only overseas but also in their own country or local community.

As you read through these pages, ask yourself if God is calling you to be involved in a special way in mission. Our hope is that this book of stories about the work of individual volunteers will inspire others to answer God's call to Christian service, whether by serving as a volunteer or by supporting prayerfully and financially those who serve.

1

The Individual
Volunteer Program

In 1735, the Georgia Trustees asked John Wesley if he and some friends would go with James Oglethorpe to the new American colony of Georgia (named for the reigning monarch) as volunteer missionaries.
—FROM THE "WESLEY IN AMERICA" EXHIBIT, PERKINS SCHOOL OF
THEOLOGY, DALLAS, TEXAS, FEBRUARY 2003

*C*hristian Love in Action," the motto of United Methodist Volunteers In Mission, is based on 1 John 3:18: "Little children, let us love, not in word or speech, but in truth and action." Living our faith is at the very heart of our Christian calling and reflects the purpose that has grown out of our understanding of who we are and what it means to put our faith into practice.

History of the Individual Volunteer Program

United Methodism has a long history of volunteer missionaries, beginning with John Wesley, the founder of Methodism, who answered God's call to travel to the colony of Georgia, where he had been invited by General James Oglethorpe to establish Anglican churches. After traveling to America, he learned Spanish in order to communicate with the Native Americans who had learned that language from the earlier Spanish explorers.

The individual volunteer program was started when some persons who had served on Volunteers In Mission teams said, "God is calling me to go by myself, not for two weeks, but for a longer time." As inquiries about how that could be done began to reach the jurisdictional UMVIM offices, a program was developed, beginning in the early 1990s, to enable persons to serve as individual volunteers for periods of two months or longer.

Others had felt God's call to mission for many years and were now ready to answer that call. As the program grew, the Southeastern Jurisdiction office of The United Methodist Church was asked to recruit, train, and place individual volunteers for the entire denomination.

By 1999 the program had expanded, and the Mission Volunteers program unit of the General Board of Global Ministries decided to sponsor the individual volunteer program for persons from the other jurisdictions in the United States and from other countries, while the Atlanta office continued to send volunteers from the Southeast.

In all this work, God has blessed the lives of many people through the service of individual volunteers. Even more, God has blessed those who have said, "Here I am, Lord. Send me."

Why Volunteer?

There are many reasons for volunteering. We will mention just a few, with stories and quotes from volunteers as illustrations.

1. "I Was Called to Be a Missionary, but..."

Martha Oldham's story is typical of the volunteers who felt God's call at a young age but were not able to fulfill it until later in life. Martha has written a book, *Africa: Lord, Hang Onto Me and Don't Let Go* (Pleasant Word, 2004). The story of her call begins with these words:

> As a small child, I felt a call to become a missionary. . . . I had always heard about my paternal grandpa Geyer's desire to be a missionary in Africa, a dream he never achieved. . . .
>
> As an adult, when I saw stories and pictures in the news showing children starving in places like Somalia and Rwanda, with refugees dying from cholera, my heart would break. . . . I wanted to go to those places and do something. (17–18)

Martha's lifelong dream was fulfilled when she joined a volunteer team organized by the United Methodist Committee on Relief (UMCOR) to work with Rwandan refugees in Bukavu, Zaire. Next was a trip to Kenya with Feed the Children, an international Christian organization based in Oklahoma City, and then to Ghana with a Volunteers In Mission team from Oklahoma. After those group experiences, she decided to apply for service as an individual volunteer in Rwanda, where she did outstanding work with women and girls who had been traumatized by the rapes, murders, and other atrocities of the genocidal war between the Hutus and the Tutsis.

2. "There's More to Life Than This . . ."

When asked, "Why do you want to be an individual volunteer?" people often reply, "I've been so blessed that I want to give something back out of gratitude to God." Especially after being exposed to poverty through a Volunteers In Mission team experience, they realize there is more to life than material blessings and want to find true meaning in their lives through service to others. A statement we have often heard is "It's payback time."

A dramatic example is the story of **Larry Cox**, who went with a volunteer team to Chile, and upon seeing the difference that volunteers can make in people's lives, decided he wanted to spend the rest of his life making that kind of difference. Several years after Larry became a full-time volunteer, his daughter **Marie** wrote a paper that sums up what the volunteer experience is all about. She wrote:

My dad was the chief financial officer and senior vice president for a flourishing company in Dallas. Now many people find it hard to believe that my dad was once a shrewd businessman, a workaholic of sorts, who worked seven days a week and had time for little else. Consequently, my family was climbing the social scale and indulging in all the amenities that accompanied our incipient wealth.

During this time, I was a happy fifth grader and I enjoyed the security of my life and family. I didn't know it, but my dad was not happy, not even close. He severely disliked the hypocrisy and tedium present in his job....

Perhaps the reason my father rejected that which he once pursued was due to his trip to Chile. The summer before he quit his job, my dad traveled to an impoverished section of Chile with a church group to build a school for the children of a small village. After my dad returned, both my mom and I could tell that the experience had changed him.

About six months later, my dad told me that he had resigned from his job. Naturally, this confused me because I thought my dad enjoyed his job; so I asked him why he would ever want to quit. I will always remember his reply: "Well, Marie, if I kept this job it would be like repeating the fifth grade over and over again." Of course, I immediately understood after he said this, for no fate would be worse for me, a fifth grader, than to repeat the fifth grade....

So how have my dad's actions affected me? He exposed me to a world that reached far beyond my white suburb. He taught me at an early age that money does not equal happiness. He showed me how to reject convention in the face of uncertainty. Truly, in a world of poverty, vice, and boredom he taught me to cultivate my garden.

Larry began his volunteer work in Dallas, Texas, as the North Texas United Methodist Volunteers In Mission coordinator. In addition to facilitating UMVIM work, he was instrumental in founding several charitable institutions to serve the needs of inner-city residents, especially immigrants and persons with handicapping conditions.

Having visited Methodist churches and social outreach programs in Matamoros, Mexico, adjacent to Brownsville, Texas, Larry decided in 2002 to leave Dallas for Matamoros, where he could be personally involved in the ministries there and help volunteers from Texas serve more effectively. The number of teams and individual volunteers Larry receives each year is phenomenal, and the stories he tells of the people who have become like family to him are amazing and inspiring.

3. "It Was a Life-changing Experience..."

Volunteers In Mission teams have often been the impetus for long-term volunteering. Dr. **Charles M. "Chuck" Wheat** described this kind of call:

> It was just ten years ago, when I came to Oklahoma to escort Mother to that year's memorial service in Dad's honor, that I first became aware of the Volunteers In Mission program. Once we had entered the church, Mother abandoned me to visit with her lifetime collection of friends, and all of my own friends disappeared into their meetings. With nothing better to do, I started scouring the tables for any sort of reading material and picked up a little flyer about a VIM mission to Costa Rica to build houses for victims of the April 1991 earthquake.
>
> I had heard somewhere that Costa Rica was a beautiful country and a tax-friendly haven for North American retirees. Since the mission in question happened to be scheduled for August, in the interim between summer school and the fall term of the university where I taught, I decided to sign up and check it out. That proved to be a truly life-changing decision—I could not have, in my wildest imagination, visualized the outcome!
>
> That first mission was in equal measure fulfilling and frustrating. Our team was highly motivated and several of the members were skilled workers, but we were frustrated by the lack of organization, sufficient materials, and an inadequate supply of tools and equipment. It was clear to me that the program could not be completed with the teams scheduled, so I asked permission to go down "solo" to do some work and help prepare for subsequent teams. Through this effort, three

17

of the houses were completed, but there were no resources available, and no teams scheduled, for the fourth house.

In my view, failing to build the fourth house would have been a tragedy—it was designated for a single lady who was caring for a young girl suffering from multiple sclerosis and confined to a wheelchair. Their nights were spent under the eave of the public library.

To get *Casa 4* (House 4) done, I organized my first team under the Mission Costa Rica flag from students in the international finance class I was teaching at Stephen F. Austin University over the 1992 spring break. Since that modest beginning, I have been blessed to work with nearly one thousand people from forty-five teams, ranging in size from seven to seventy-four members (averaging about twenty-two), in several major projects. [Authors' note: The total number of teams and volunteers has now more than doubled.]

Bob May, who later became a missionary with the United Methodist General Board of Global Ministries, inquired about becoming an individual volunteer after he served on a Volunteers In Mission team. Because he was a highly skilled computer professional, we told him about the need for someone to go to the Philippines to help install computers in a United Methodist seminary and university, and teach faculty and staff how to use them.

When he came to the orientation/training session, Bob told the other volunteers that he was leaving his job in the computer industry to spend several months volunteering because he wanted to recapture the deeply satisfying emotions of the volunteer experience. "It was the greatest experience of my life," he said, "and I wanted it to continue on and on."

Bob stayed in the Philippines even longer than he had planned, thanks to financial help from church members back home in Virginia. He eventually returned home and notified us that he was ready to volunteer again. We had just received a request for someone to upgrade the computer system for an ecumenical mission agency in Afghanistan, and, of course, Bob was the ideal person for that task. At the time, since the Taliban was in control of the country, we could not tell others where he was assigned. He was listed as serving in Central Asia. His experiences there were so compelling that when his work was completed he applied to become a full-time missionary and was accepted, serving first in Bethlehem (Israel/Palestine) and more recently in Tonga, teaching computer classes at Queen Salote College.

4. "I Saw It on the Internet..."

Volunteers sometimes apply for a specific position they have seen advertised on the Mission Volunteers website (http://gbgm-umc.org/vim) or in a national or regional church publication, because it seems to be something for which they are well suited and would enjoy doing for a few months or longer.

A dramatic response to a specific need occurred one January when we received a request for a volunteer pastor to serve an English-speaking congregation in Milan, Italy, while the pastor was on sabbatical. We placed a notice in *Newscope*, a national United Methodist newsletter, and it was picked up and published by the Minnesota Conference UMVIM newsletter. We received more than sixty inquiries about the position in sunny Italy, most of them from icy Minnesota. A retired North Texas Conference evangelist was assigned to Milan, but a Minnesota pastor went to the *Casa Materna* orphanage in Naples and served there for several years as a result of sending her application to go to Milan.

On another occasion God sent us the perfect volunteer for a difficult assignment in the Democratic Republic of the Congo. The United Methodist Committee on Relief requested a French-speaking volunteer architect or building contractor to help build covered market-places in that war-torn country so that people in the villages could begin to rebuild their local economy.

Shortly after we placed the request on the Mission Volunteers website, we had a reply from **Dominique Gettliffe** of Boulder, Colorado. Dominique is an architect and building contractor, originally from France, who had been searching for something meaningful to do in addition to his work building homes for affluent Americans—something that would help people who could not afford to repay him. The request from UMCOR sounded as if it had been written specifically for him. We heard from Dominique just a few days before our next scheduled orientation/training, to be held in Dulac, Louisiana, and on very short notice he arranged to be there.

The training weekend itself was a confirmation of God's call for Dominique. We found that the people served by the Dulac Community Center, where we held the training, are Houma Indians whose first language is French. After attending their French-speaking church service on Sunday, Dominique enjoyed visiting with the pastor and other church members who were thrilled to find that one of our volunteers spoke their native language.

Several times we have received a request for a librarian. Iquique English College, a bilingual Methodist elementary and high school in northern Chile, asked for a librarian who could help them computerize the library. We had just received an application from a retired librarian, **Elizabeth Parker** of Wichita, Kansas, and asked her about going to Chile. She said she could not do that because her mother would not want her to leave the United States. We found a place for Elizabeth at Lon Morris College, a United Methodist institution in Jacksonville, Texas, and later she served at the Servants in Faith and Technology (SIFAT) center in Lineville, Alabama, and at Henderson Settlement in Frakes, Kentucky.

5. *"I'm Glad You Asked..."*

Some persons have studied the list of opportunities for individual volunteers found on the Internet and have been led to apply for a specific position listed. Others say, "Here I am, Lord. Send me wherever you will. I want to go where the need is the greatest."

Sometimes we have received a request from a specific location and shortly thereafter a person has called who is interested in serving anywhere, and we have said, "This request has just come in. How does that sound to you?" It has been thrilling to fill a need that has just been shared with us, although it is equally satisfying to find a volunteer for a position that has been on the list for a long time.

Volunteers often hear God's call in person, through someone who tells about a need for volunteers. In August 2004, a missionary in Honduras spoke for about fifteen minutes to a large group of volunteers and former volunteers at a combination orientation/training/reunion at the Wilderness Retreat and Development Center in Lawson, Missouri. Later, several persons who had heard the missionary volunteered in Honduras. Hearing of the needs from someone who had recently been there made the mission challenge come alive for them.

At another orientation/training weekend, held in August 2000 at the Cabrini Retreat Center in Des Plaines, Illinois, we had invited Reverend **José Pulgar**, a retired pastor from Chile, to come and speak to the volunteers. José's wife, **Carris Hughes**, grew up in a Welsh colony in Argentina. The couple had served an exchange pastorate in Wales and had done pastoral work in Argentina and Chile, and they were willing to share their experiences of working in different cultural settings.

We returned home to find a request from the General Board of Global Ministries for a volunteer to replace a missionary coming to the United States for six months. The missionary was the area financial executive and the coordinator for Volunteers In Mission teams in Bolivia. José Pulgar, having had experience with volunteers in Chile and having been a district superintendent, seemed to be the ideal person for the job, so we sent him a special invitation to apply as an individual volunteer.

José and Carris were still in the Chicago area visiting their daughter, and José sent us his application immediately. He had his references faxed from Chile, and we received the paperwork and approved him as a volunteer within a week's time. Providentially, he had already attended the training, so after returning to Chile to arrange for someone to care for their home, he and Carris were soon in Bolivia, where José did an outstanding job.

Constance Waddell described a similar life-changing encounter. Her husband, the Reverend **Don Waddell**, is a retired pastor and former missionary in Chile. She wrote:

> Some of you may not know that Don and I have volunteered at El Tabo *Campamento* (Camp) for two years.... We were in the Chilean missionary reunion in Portland, Oregon, when Betty and Walt Whitehurst said a couple was needed to help restore the camp.
>
> Bishop Grandón, newly elected Bishop of Chile, and his wife, Silvia, were there for the reunion. I thought when we talked with him about coming that Don would say, "I have diabetes and neuropathy and have had a heart attack in the past and prostate cancer surgery in the recent past, and sit most of the time in a recliner, so how could I go?"
>
> Instead, he said to me, "Let's go to the room and talk and pray about this." I was in agreement, and although this was August, Don was on his way to Chile by September 17—in time to celebrate *Dieciocho* [September 18, Chile's Independence Day].... I came a month and a half later.
>
> *It is wonderful.... It is also a challenge....* It is wonderful in the sense that Don has been almost *well*—he has been outdoors and working and eager to talk with people and just loving it all. It has been wonderful to breathe the fresh air and see the ocean at a distance and now and then go to the beach.

Who Are the Individual Volunteers?

Individual volunteers are persons who respond to God's call to serve in a mission setting in the United States or some other country. They are committed Christians, young and old and in between, who feel richly blessed and want to share their time and talents to help others. Most are from the United States, but some are from other countries. They are usually single adults or married couples, although some go as families with children.

Young persons may wish to spend several months, or a year or more, in volunteer service before completing their studies or beginning their careers. Mid-career persons sometimes take a leave of absence in order to volunteer for a significant period of time. Many retired persons choose to be long-term individual volunteers out of gratitude for blessings received throughout their lives.

Each individual volunteer is unique, and every volunteer placement is different from all others. Nevertheless, we would like to present certain categories to demonstrate the breadth of life experiences represented.

1. Young Adults

Younger volunteers serve in the United States beginning at age eighteen and may serve in other countries at age twenty-one or after two years of college or work experience away from home. They are among the most dedicated and enthusiastic volunteers, and many have received high praise from the people under whom they have worked.

Jasmine Miller, coordinator of volunteers at McCurdy School in Espanola, New Mexico, was herself a long-term individual volunteer. She was somewhat doubtful about receiving **Allie Miller** (no relation to Jasmine), a college student from Kalamazoo, Michigan, because Allie would be the only young person among the large volunteer community at McCurdy. Jasmine wrote:

> I am going ahead with Allie's application. My only concern is the lack of volunteers her age. We will not even have student teachers during that time. I did explain that to Allie and her mother at the orientation/training weekend in Iowa. I will be visiting with principals about her this week.

For Allie, being the only young volunteer was not an obstacle to enjoying her time in New Mexico. She wrote upon her arrival:

> So here I am—my last night before I start at the school! I arrived here Friday night safe and sound, to my mom's amazement! The other volunteers kept me busy that weekend, going to the high school basketball game, the San Idlefonso pueblo, and touring Santa Fe. There are several United Methodist churches that were started in this area

after McCurdy was started, and on Sunday we attended a small one forty-five minutes from Espanola.

Well into her two months of volunteering, Allie's enthusiasm had not diminished:

> I am still really enjoying my time down here. I am constantly amazed at the dedication of the McCurdy staff. And I love this area! It has been so sunny... but I think I've been bragging about it too much because it got cold this weekend, and we also got about two inches of rain. Everyone is very excited about that.
>
> I only have three weeks left! There is so much going on with school, field trips, plays, etc. And this week is full of Holy Week things, which is very exciting—a Seder meal, a pilgrimage to Chimayo (about eight miles away), a Good Friday service that I'm in—the youth group is doing it, and then a sunrise Easter service! I am excited.

Young adults have enjoyed serving in many different ways in a variety of locations, as the following examples indicate.

After completing graduate school, **Kristin Grauer** was accepted by the U.S. State Department for diplomatic service. While waiting for her assignment, she chose to go to Poland to teach English as an individual volunteer. Midway through the semester she was called to report to Washington, D.C., to begin her work as a diplomat. She was torn between God's call to continue her mission service and her dream of an international career, and was greatly relieved when a volunteer English teacher from New Zealand was found to take her place teaching English. It may have been a somewhat confusing change for the Polish students, since the New Zealand accent and Kristin's Midwestern United States accent were two distinct versions of English pronunciation.

Mindy Buchanan, a college student from Texas, was a summer volunteer at a United Methodist camp in France. She wrote: "Never washed so many dishes, made so many beds, fed so many people in my life! Mopping, sweeping, everything. Not the most glamorous of jobs, but I've learned to find joy in being a servant of Christ in a new way. Amazing!"

2. Mid-Career Volunteers

Many individual volunteers are persons who have taken time to volunteer during their working years. **Cheryl Lafferty** and **Howard Pisons**, who left their successful positions in the business world to teach at Iquique English College in northern Chile for a year, are a good example of these mid-career volunteers. Returning to the United States, Howard found a position in a financial firm in Richmond, Virginia, and Cheryl taught Spanish until their twins were born and she became a stay-at-home mom.

Cheryl wrote about their volunteer work:

> It has been almost twelve weeks since we started teaching. Some weeks are difficult because of a number of factors: communication difficulty, discipline of some of the children, many obligations, and little time to rest. Within all of this the real question was: How are we going to choose to handle this?
>
> Our involvement has grown past teaching:
>
> We have started an English Club here at the school. One for seventh and eighth graders and one for high schoolers. All ideas are welcomed!
>
> We lead the youth group at church (fifth through eighth graders) and meet every Sunday.
>
> We teach English to the professors and administrators once a week.
>
> Howard works with the kids in intramural basketball three times a week. He's had to learn a whole new vocabulary for coaching and refereeing.

Sung Kim, who worked for a computer firm in New Jersey, spent a year in an Asian country where his computer expertise made him a welcome guest even in a place where Christian mission is officially forbidden. He willingly did even more than his position required, as a silent witness to the love of Christ:

Currently, I'm teaching computer at the computer center in the National University. This computer center was set up in the foreign language department by the organization I'm associated with.

Though I'm learning the local language, I'm teaching in English for English major students (only eight people in the class). I had one session (eight-week schedule) already and am doing the second session. Working with young people is always exciting and interesting. Since I'm teaching just Microsoft Office, it's not difficult to teach.

I also teach English for some students by the request of a friend. They are medical students, trying to enter the one-year seminar program provided by a small hospital with Korean doctors. Since the seminar is taught in English, the students will have to pass an English test/interview. These medical students are God's children, and they belong to my friend's group, so I'm just helping them in whatever possible way.

During a time when the United Methodist General Board of Global Ministries was not sending new missionaries, some persons who felt called to mission service applied to become individual volunteers because the career missionary option was not available. The Reverend **Paul Shew**, who wanted to serve in Japan, was able to do so thanks to being recognized as an official individual volunteer, accepted by the Council on Cooperative Mission in Japan as a missionary associate.

Paul kept us informed about the process:

I am currently seeking an appointment to Aoyama Gakuin University as a missionary to serve as both teaching faculty and chaplain. Aoyama Gakuin, located in Tokyo, is a highly regarded Methodist-related school, incorporating a complete educational system from kindergarten through doctoral programs.

The leadership of Aoyama Gakuin University is vitally concerned with preserving their Methodist heritage and using education as a means to witnessing to the gospel of Jesus Christ.... They want someone who can serve as both chaplain and teaching faculty, and who can represent The United Methodist Church as a missionary....

After a lengthy hiring process, I am happy to report that Aoyama Gakuin University has officially welcomed me as an assistant professor, chaplain, and missionary....

It's good to see the church in America (through the faithful people at VIM) responding to the desires of the church in Japan and working to meet their needs.

3. *Volunteer Families*

Another facet of our work with volunteers has been helping families to be in mission. We were supportive of this idea because we had served as a missionary family in Chile, and subsequently our children were a part of the Volunteers In Mission teams we took to Mexico and Chile.

The Porter family from British Columbia, Canada, was the first volunteer family we helped to place. **Rob and Pam Porter** and their children, **Celia and Drew**, asked about volunteering for several months in the Democratic Republic of the Congo. Because Rob knew French, it seemed an ideal place for them. We had made the arrangements for them to go there, and they had purchased their tickets, when a rebellion began that made it impossible for them to travel to the Congo.

Through the United Methodist connectional system, we were able to quickly find a volunteer assignment for them in Ghana. Shortly after their return home, Pam wrote about their volunteer experience:

> Celia tried out the neighborhood Catholic school. Then Drew tried it too. It was the best school in Sunyani, yet there were no books or toilets. With more than fifty children in each class, maintaining order was difficult. Crowds formed when Celia or Drew opened a math workbook or paperback novel.
>
> Twice a week, Selah arrived to wash our clothes. She pulled two enormous pans from under a table in the kitchen and took the clothes out to the yard where she slapped shirts together, pitted underwear against towels, and bleached colors to mediocrity. There were casualties. Some required stitches.
>
> Her brother Thomas, a tailor, would appear at unexpected moments at the school, in the middle of a city street, or in front of the vegetable stands and ask if everything was all right. We called him our angel.

Celia and Drew said he had the biggest smile they'd ever seen. He sewed for us Ghanaian outfits and a special, surprise shirt and dress for Drew and Celia.

Scott and Susan Wiggans, spending a year in Fiji with their four children, wrote shortly before Christmas:

> Our greetings this year are from halfway around the world. We are spending a year in Fiji, volunteering our time at the Dilkusha Children's Home, a home for abandoned, abused, and neglected children. . . .
>
> Although English (actually the British/Australian version) is the primary language spoken in Fiji, we hear lots of Fijian, Hindi, and other South Pacific languages. We want to share with you some words that we have added to our vocabulary here:
>
> *Lollies:* Abigail, now three years old, always seems to have a supply of these small candies that are given to her by the very friendly people here!
>
> *Hee:* Andrew, six and a half, regularly plays this involved game of tag at school where he just completed Class 1 (first grade). He had a tough adjustment to his new school, but now enjoys playing with his thirty-eight other classmates.
>
> *Net Ball:* Rachel, nine and in Class 3, enjoys playing a basketball-like game (without dribbling) on Fridays, which is Sports Day at school.
>
> *Pawpaw:* Elizabeth, eleven and a half and in Class 6, loves picking and eating the papaya that grow on the Home and school grounds. Fruits are plentiful in Fiji, and she also likes the curry dishes and *roti* (flat bread).
>
> *Sulu:* Susan wears these beautiful wraparound skirts to church and special occasions. On most other days, she works with the special-needs children at the Home, enjoying getting her hands back into the physical therapy field. She also spends time reading and playing with the nursery children and helping the elementary-age schoolchildren with homework. All that fits around daily living and caring for our family, including evenings often spent bathing children, treating infections, and pulling lice and nits out of hair.
>
> *Bure:* Scott has done several handyman projects under this type of roof on our front porch—out of the hot sun and rain. He built and re-

paired many items around the Home complex and has started the design of a new covered playground structure (with lots of interest and "assistance" from the children). He is also teaching computer and job application skills to the older girls, staff, and a growing group of community members. He and Susan each lead an evening devotion one night per week at the Home.

Later, they wrote again to describe the family's reactions to their time in Fiji, in the form of answers to questions:

Besides friends and family, what do you miss about Colorado?
Elizabeth, 11: A bedroom without my brother, and our backyard.
Rachel, 9: Our school playground, hot showers, and church choir.
Andrew, 6: Boys, my room, toys, and playing sports.
Abigail, 3: The zoo, snow, a big bathtub, and short church services.
Scott: A well-stocked hardware store, reliable computers, boneless meat, and a car.
Susan: Family privacy, a large refrigerator/freezer, and e-mail in the house.
Besides the people, what will you miss about Fiji?
Elizabeth: Walking to school and eating all the fruits.
Rachel: Having so many friends close by.
Andrew: Lots of playtime with my dad, and fresh pineapple.
Abigail: Preschool, lots of extra big "sisters."
Scott: Having a less-stressful schedule, lush green vegetation, and nearby ocean.
Susan: Beautiful singing and hearing eight hundred schoolgirls reciting the Lord's Prayer.

The Meyer family from Oregon provided a different kind of family involvement. **Julie Meyer**, after graduating from college and before entering law school, volunteered for a year in Bolivia. Then her brother **Jacob**, between college and medical school, spent several months as a volunteer in Peru. Finally, their older sister **Stephanie**, a public-school music teacher, volunteered for a year in Chile. Each of them was visited by other family members, including their parents, during the time they served as volunteers. All of them were out-standing volunteers, doing far more than the job description they agreed to when they accepted their assignments, because of their concern for human rights and for helping people find ways to live in dignity and escape from poverty.

Julie was asked to teach English at Río Colorado Methodist School in Bolivia, but she also discovered a nearby group of indigenous people, the Tsimanes, and began working with them in addition to teaching in Río Colorado. She wrote about one activity with the Tsimane children:

> I want to tell everyone about a field trip we recently planned with the Tsimane School. I spent more money ($20–$25) in order to plan the trip, since there is no money available here for luxuries like field trips. The excitement of the kids made it worth it, and I wish you could have seen them as they climbed into the truck that we used to go to Rurre....
>
> We left Wednesday morning at five o'clock. I had the kids divided into four pickup points along the road.... By the time we picked up all the kids and left, it was six thirty. We had twenty-four kids from Bajo Colorado and eighteen from San Martín....
>
> We arrived in Rurre and immediately went to the mayor's office, where the staff was waiting for us. My kids sang and then asked questions we had prepared the week before. Since Thursday was *"Día del Niño"* (Children's Day), another school was in the *plaza* doing a treasure hunt. When the mayor told the kids to join in, I about died! There were over a hundred kids swarming in the *plaza*, and we would have probably lost ours in the chaos.
>
> Luckily, the kids were overwhelmed and didn't stray far from the adults. We herded them to one more government office and also to the school district office (a two-room adobe hut with open windows).... There are four thousand kids in the district and four persons in the office. No computers and no telephone....
>
> After the office visits, we took the kids to lunch at a *pensión* (a restaurant that serves a set menu). The owners had agreed to serve a complete lunch for three *bolivianos* per child (less than fifty cents).... After lunch came the real treat that everyone was waiting for. We took all of them to San Buenaventura, the little town on the other side of *Río Beni* (the Beni

River). We crossed in the ferry, much to their delight.... They played soccer in a beautiful little *plaza* surrounded by palm trees. Thankfully, we only had one bruised shin. I bought the little boy ice (a precious commodity here) to put on the bump, and within ten minutes he ate it all!

We crossed the river again to board our luxurious pickup truck. We ran a little late, but we had the last child dropped off by eight thirty. All of the parents were waiting by the side of the road to pick up their children. I was exhausted, mostly from worrying that I would lose a student, but it was all worth it.

Jacob was assigned to assist the district superintendent in Huancayo, Peru, with Methodist work throughout the district. In addition to working in the churches, Jacob was able to help establish a market for hand-knitted items made by the women, to enable them to provide income for their households. Jacob shared with us some of his experiences during his time in Peru:

Saturdays in the morning I have my Quechua class. In the afternoon I go to San Carlos, which is a neighborhood of Huancayo, to teach a Bible study and the literacy class. This is probably my favorite time of the week. I visit two or three of the members of this group every week. They are all very hospitable and serve me tea or pancakes (fried dough) and we talk about the church, the Bible, family, life in Peru, life in the United States, their children, and any other random thing. Next week they are all coming over to my house to cook dinner together. In the group, there are about twelve women and one man. Myself, I think I'll be doing more learning than cooking.

Stephanie went to La Granja, an agricultural school for Mapuche Indian children in southern Chile, to teach music. She became aware of other needs, including starting a sports program for girls and helping establish an herb garden project to generate income for the school. She was very much loved by the students, faculty, and staff. A volunteer who went to La Granja the following year asked in an e-mail, "Who is Stephanie? Everyone here asks me 'How is Stephanie? When is Stephanie coming back?' "

Stephanie wrote about some of her experiences from her time in Chile:

> I started teaching today. The music teacher is out of town, so I am taking his schedule this week. I know now that this school is going to be perfect. I felt so comfortable and welcome....
>
> The best part that shocked me was when I walked in the room for the first time, they all stood up and waited silently until I told them to take their seats! What a change, eh?
>
> They bore with me as I tried (and failed) to pronounce all their names. I am the only foreign teacher, and the other teachers are Chilean. The kids all come from the countryside and are Mapuche Indians, so many of them speak *Mapudungun*. I have tried to learn some words, but it is hard. . . . For now I will concentrate on the Spanish.

We will leave the final word about the Meyer family volunteers to **Nancy Meyer**, mother of Julie, Jacob, and Stephanie. Nancy wrote, following a visit she and her husband, Walter, made to see Stephanie in Chile, about a major surprise God had planned for them there:

> Stephanie attended an ecumenical worship service a few weeks ago at a Catholic church. The priest was talking about Jesus and the disciples being in the boat during the storm and how the disciples were afraid. The priest told the people to turn for a moment and talk with someone sitting close to them about fears they might have.
>
> Stephanie was sitting in front of a couple our age. The woman told her that she was afraid of being alone. Her children were grown and her youngest son (Eduardo and his wife, Patricia) recently left Chile to live in the United States. Stephanie told her that she was from the United States and wondered where her son was. She told Stephie that he was living in Oregon. Stephanie said, "Really? I'm from Oregon. What city?"
>
> The woman replied, "Eugene"! It turns out that her son and his wife live within walking distance of our house! They invited Stephanie to dinner and to meet Patricia's parents, who were planning a trip to Eugene to visit. When they found out that we lived in Eugene they even took a video of Stephanie to bring with them.
>
> We invited Eduardo, Patricia, and her parents for dinner Sunday night and had a wonderful time. What a small world. God is working overtime in our family!

4. Retirees

Many retired persons, usually self-financed by their retirement income, serve as volunteers in the United States and abroad. We would like to share some of their stories.

Alice and Rock Rothrock were already volunteering at Dulac Community Center in Houma, Louisiana, when we went there for an individual volunteer orientation/training weekend in February 2004. They signed up as individual volunteers through our program shortly after we were there. They wrote about the beginning of their volunteer experience, almost twelve years earlier: "Late October of 1992 is when we first came to Dulac. They stole our hearts right away, and now we have gotten rid of all our real estate and most other encumbrances and are here as long as God allows us to be useful. It's a great place to be."

In May 2008, having retired from Dulac Community Center, they wrote: "We are still involved as individual volunteers in our home church, First United Methodist Church in Orange, Texas. We help with the hurricane repair of the storm of 2005, Christian services food pantry, and exhort others to be involved. We think we will never be too old to volunteer."

Dave and Jan Calley of Colby, Wisconsin, had been on a Volunteers In Mission team in the Caribbean. On the way there, they traveled through Antigua and visited the Gilbert Center, where Methodism began in the Caribbean, and saw potential for use of the center for VIM teams in the area. They applied to go back there to help coordinate work teams going to Antigua and other locations served by The Methodist Church of the Caribbean and the Americas. However, their placement there was taking a long time to arrange, and we were not sure it was going to be a possibility.

When we received a notice that the Midwest Mission Distribution Center (MMDC) in Chatham, Illinois, needed a couple to serve as directors of the center, we recommended to Dave and Jan that they apply. They did and were chosen to fill that position.

33

Well into their work there, Dave and Jan wrote about their experience:

> Here it is, more than six months into our year's commitment as directors at the Midwest Mission Distribution Center. It seems like yesterday when we arrived on a cold winter day. The mission of the center continues to grow. New contacts provide opportunities to serve the less fortunate of the world. Orphan Grain Train of Norfolk, Nebraska, and Medical Bridges of Houston, Texas, have enabled the MMDC to send donations of medical equipment and supplies to countries such as Argentina, India, and Pakistan.

One category of retirees that has provided outstanding individual volunteers is that of retired missionaries.

Reverend **Leta Gorham** of Plano, Texas, has volunteered in the Democratic Republic of the Congo, where she and her late husband were missionaries for many years, then in Nepal, and more recently in Korea.

Below are some of her reflections. From Nepal:

> What a journey of discovery this period of my life continues to be! What a joy—what a challenge! It seems that every moment I am called to confront my faith—the belief system in which I grew up and took for granted. There are no symbols of my faith here—no crosses, no doves. But on every corner there is a temple covered with red powder and flower petals and bells to ring to summon a god, and at most every house there is a small worship center.
>
> The greatest gift we expatriate Christians have to give is to live each day as though it may be our last, to show how our God is always a God of love and a God of hope.

From Korea:

> Five o'clock morning prayer seven days a week on these worn-out, scarred knees and joints that cry out when bent—it's quite a way to start the day in God's love.... The "music" of the voices of the people all praying at once reminds me again of how our one God can hear and respond to each one of us.

George and Yoko Gish, recently retired missionaries in Japan, arranged to continue their missionary work by becoming individual volunteers. George wrote:

> On my birthday, we attended the Christmas service and party for the faculty and staff of Toyo Eiwa Girls School, where I had been asked to give the message. In speaking of our task of reconciliation as a response to God's love, I shared how we felt when we stood at Ground Zero in New York last month during our visit for recognition of our retirement as United Methodist Church missionaries. I mentioned that for us, the tragedy of 9/11 was a vivid reminder of the continuation of the sufferings that took place at Hiroshima, Nagasaki, and the saturation bombings of Tokyo in 1945.
>
> When we sat at the front table for the party after the worship service, the man sitting next to us happened to be the principal of the high school. He mentioned how grateful he was that I had referred to the bombing of Tokyo, because both of his parents had been killed on that terrible night when some one hundred thousand people lost their lives during the intensive bombing of the old section of Tokyo that was the most densely populated. When Yoko asked how he had been raised, he said he was thankful for his grandparents who had taken him in. We both renewed our vows to work for peace through the education of the next generation of youth.

Retirees also include persons with motor homes who travel from one volunteer opportunity in the United States to another. Some have participated in the group volunteer experience known as NOMADS (Nomads On a Mission Active in Divine Service), a rapidly growing organization that had its origin as a program of United Methodist Volunteers In Mission, North Central Jurisdiction, and have decided to volunteer for longer than the three-week NOMADS assignments.

Others, upon their retirement, have purchased a motor home instead of a house, freeing them to travel and to volunteer wherever and whenever they are needed. **Hal and Margaret Waters** served in this way for many years, alternating between church projects and volunteering in the National Park system:

Our volunteer service with the United States Forest Service near Albuquerque was so enjoyable that we have agreed to return in a year. This is also true of our two-week stay at McCurdy Mission School in Espanola, New Mexico, where Margaret was a third-grade teacher's aide and Hal built a new roof over the kindergarten and coordinated a major relocation to other quarters of administration and home economics.....

One year after retirement, we can evaluate our decisions somewhat objectively. We are satisfied that our decisions were right. We are extremely happy with our new lifestyle, our mobile abode, and our chosen career of volunteer service. We do not miss our disposed possessions and other encumbrances. We have all the necessary items to be self-sufficient. Sometimes we find our physical and mental endurance taxed to the maximum, but we believe that to be superior to decaying and rotting in place!

5. Volunteers from Outside the United States

It has been our privilege to work with persons from outside the United States who wanted to volunteer through our program, although such placements are more difficult to arrange due to visa regulations and lack of financial assistance. The Walt and Betty Whitehurst Individual Volunteers Scholarship Fund has been established by the Mission Volunteers office of the General Board of Global Ministries (Advance Special #982465-6, earmarked "Individual Volunteers Scholarship Fund") so that anyone who wishes may help provide financial assistance to volunteers from other countries whose congregations and families are not able to pay the volunteers' expenses.

Although the number of international volunteers has remained small, those who have participated in our program have given outstanding volunteer service. We have enjoyed working with a young woman from the Netherlands who volunteered in Chile, a Mexican volunteer who went to Bolivia, Chileans serving in El Salvador and Bolivia, volunteers in Cambodia from Zimbabwe and Finland, a Fijian pastor living in Seattle who returned to Fiji as a volunteer, a Korean computer engineer living in the United States who spent a year with his family in Central Asia, and volunteers coming to the United States from Bolivia and the Philippines.

A news release describing the work of **Modesta Kalaw**, a deaconess from the Philippines who volunteered in the United States, was issued by the General Board of Global Ministries in March 2001 and was later included in the *Stories of Individual Volunteers* section of the Mission Volunteers website (http://gbgm-umc.org/vim):

> The first volunteer from another country to be assigned to service as an individual volunteer in the United States is close to completing a four-month term of mission service in Florida.
>
> Modesta Kalaw of Tarlac City, the Philippines, says that as she comes closer to God and depends on his love and protection, "I become more sensitive to the needs of the least of my brothers and sisters around me."
>
> She says she is grateful for the opportunity to live her faith during her four months of mission service as a volunteer. Through her work with children and adults at the Carver Heights Ministry in Leesburg, Florida, Kalaw says she is gaining skills and experience that she can take back to the Philippines. A United Methodist deaconess and the mother of seven children, Kalaw taught elementary grades and preschool at the Tarlac Ecumenical School in the Philippines. She was granted a leave of absence to do missionary work in the Florida Conference....
>
> Kalaw's mission service began in January in Coral Gables, Florida, where she worked for two months as an assistant at the Growing Place preschool of the First United Methodist Church. She also helped distribute tracts and the Upper Room devotional booklets on campus for the Wesley Foundation of the University of Miami.

The following excerpts are from correspondence sent by other volunteers from outside the United States.

Ana María López, a Bolivian serving in Virginia, wrote in an e-mail to other volunteers:

> I'm volunteering here in Virginia.... Recently I visited three different Hispanic churches. I could see they need a lot of help. I am going

to help with Sunday school and hope to help in many ways. Many people don't have jobs, and there are lots of children with many needs, but most of them come to the church, so they want to follow Jesus. Pray for the Hispanic ministries and the people who are in charge.

Reverend **José Pulgar**, a Chilean volunteer, made the following observations about his work in Bolivia:

Things are going very well here. I have a lot of work since church takes up my Sundays. I preach as many as three times in one day. Lately, because we are celebrating the Month of Methodism, I have been asked to give talks in the American School and in church gatherings. Last night I was in two panel discussions about Methodism, first with 250 students in the night school who are studying accounting for adults, and later with 300 in another session. Tomorrow I will give the keynote address about Methodism in a gathering of all the churches of La Paz and of the district, at ten o'clock in the morning, in the gymnasium of the American School.

In the church office I work with an excellent team, including a secretary and accountant, and the work has become routine so that I know by memory the rules, projects, and entire work process. I am happy here, and probably there will be tears when I leave. I have made very good friends, and I have the impression that everyone is pleased with my presence and my work.

I am taking a ninety-minute class of advanced English every day. I leave at 6:30 in the morning for the American-Bolivian Institute. There is no bus at that time, so I walk thirty minutes, up and down hills, and begin the class at 7:15 and finish at 8:45. I return by taxi and arrive exactly at 9:00 to open the office. On Monday, Wednesday, and Friday evenings I go to a gymnasium from 6:00 to 7:00 for a workout on their special equipment. All of this keeps me busy. As a good Methodist, I keep a very "methodical" schedule.

Preparation for Volunteer Service

Young and old, clergy and lay, men and women and children—volunteers are ordinary people called by God to do extraordinary things.

The steps they follow in order to become individual volunteers, sponsored by the Mission Volunteers unit of the United Methodist General
Board of Global Ministries, are described below.

1. The Application Process

Specific dates of service depend on when the volunteer is available and when the host community would like for the volunteer to
serve. In many countries, fluency in the language is required. Once the
Mission Volunteers office receives the application, references, and
medical form, consultations take place, usually by telephone. Then
the application is sent to the applicant's first choice of location. If that
placement does not materialize, the application may be sent to other
places. The volunteer and the office agree on the locations to be con-
sidered. This process often takes several months.

Before volunteers leave on assignment, they must attend to many
details. They should consider what will need to be done by a trusted
friend or family member while they are away, and they must plan for
spending an extended time in a new location.

To facilitate planning, it is helpful for the volunteer to be in close
touch with the person who will be supervising the volunteer's work.
A letter from one potential volunteer, **Donna Nassoiy Darling**, to the
missionary in Cambodia with whom she was to serve, is a good il-
lustration of the kind of preparation volunteers need to make before
beginning their term of service:

> Greetings to you in the name of our compassionate Lord, Jesus!
> You do not know me yet, but I am planning to join you in June as an
> individual volunteer. I will be arriving as part of the team led by War-
> ren and Jo Harbert and will stay on in Siem Reap after their departure.
> I will remain there until October 1. I have been invited to come and
> work with the children and youth program.
>
> I have never been to Cambodia. I do not speak Khmer. But I be-
> lieve I was called by God to come there, and I am being obedient
> to that call. I have a thousand questions!... I will list some of my

immediate questions at this time, and if you can answer them or direct me as to where I can get answers, great!

1. Where am I going to live? Who should I contact to make these arrangements and determine expenses?

2. What will I be doing? What kind of materials do you suggest I bring? I don't know how rough the situation is or how limited you are for basic kinds of materials/supplies. Any particular cultural issues I should be aware of as I gather information and materials for youth and children?

3. What should I do about money? Should I open a bank account; bring credit cards, travelers checks, and cash; or have family members wire money as I need it? How expensive will it be to live there? The invitation I received indicated that about $200 per month should be sufficient.

You should know that I am studying Khmer. I won't be fluent by any means! But I thought that familiarizing myself with the language would help me pick it up more quickly once I arrive. I am excited and looking forward to meeting and working with you!

2. Financing the Mission

Individual volunteers are responsible for their own financial support. Some volunteers pay their own expenses, having saved money for that purpose or having a source of income that will support them in their mission work. Those who have retirement income may find that the cost of living as a volunteer is less than their previous expenses have been, so that even with the extra travel expense they are able to break even. Some are financed by their local churches or by friends and relatives. Others find creative ways of financing their volunteer experience.

A young woman, upon completing her studies at Duke University, sent graduation invitations to her family and friends with a note asking them not to give her a gift but inviting them to donate to a fund to pay her expenses for a year as a volunteer teacher in a Methodist school in Honduras. She was given more than enough to meet her needs and was able to donate some of the money to the school.

A young adult from a very large church in Texas was having trouble getting enough financial assistance for her six months in Costa Rica until she wrote to her grandparents, members of a very small church in North Carolina, whose congregation raised the amount she needed in record time.

Some volunteers serve repeatedly for a few months at a time, and find a job after each mission assignment to earn enough money for their next volunteer venture. **Don White**, a sculptor, former community college instructor, and lay pastor in the Church of the Nazarene, returns after volunteer assignments to his home in New Mexico, where commissioned works of wood sculpture have provided financing for each successive volunteer venture.

After his time in El Salvador, before going to Bethehem (Israel/Palestine), Don wrote to us from New Mexico:

> For the next three months I've a large wood sculpture to complete for a patron in Texas.... To fill in my spare minutes I am also sculpting a wax bear for future casting, carving a fancy walnut cane for a friend, and refinishing two captain's chairs for the parsonage. Now if the cold weather will just wait until I'm ready to exit!

Even more unusual is the story told by **Martha Oldham** in her book *Africa: Lord, Hang Onto Me and Don't Let Go* (114–16) about how she was able to finance her mission work in Rwanda during her trip to Baldwin, Louisiana, for the Individual Volunteer Orientation/Training in November 1999:

> In the 1960s I bought two paintings by Clementine Hunter, a primitive artist in the historic town of Natchitoches, the oldest permanent settlement in the Louisiana Purchase. I gave $25 each for them....
> I took those paintings to sell, as I knew there would be a market in Natchitoches.... After my friend called the bank president...we learned he had a board member who was looking for Clementine's paintings....
> "How much do you want for them?" she asked....

"Make me an offer and I will take them to an antique store and see what they will say."

"I will give you $4,000 for them."

It was all I could do for my mouth not to drop open. I figured they were worth a couple of hundred dollars. "You just bought them," I said.

3. Orientation/Training

Orientation/training for individual volunteers is offered four times a year in different parts of the United States. Each event begins on Friday afternoon and ends at noon on Sunday. The weekend is filled with activities: Bible study, theologies of mission, cross-cultural adaptation, health and safety, and practical tips for mission preparation.

At each orientation/training there are young, middle-aged, and older volunteers. Some are just beginning the application process; others are preparing to leave for their volunteer assignments immediately. Some plan to volunteer for as little as two months, others for a year or longer. Some will volunteer in the United States, some in other countries. Yet after a few hours together there is a feeling of unity and an assurance of mutual support and understanding that are possible only through the presence of the Holy Spirit.

At an evaluation time at the end of each session, we almost always hear from the young volunteers how impressed they are that the older people are still so active and involved in mission, and from the older volunteers words of praise for the young people's willingness to offer their time and talents in the Lord's service.

Another recurring statement has been that although participating in Bible study and intercultural awareness exercises and learning about the practical issues of volunteering were very important, the best thing about the weekend was getting to know the other volunteers and forming a close-knit group that would continue to support one another through prayer and correspondence, especially e-mail, so that no one would feel alone in the volunteer experience.

Once the volunteers begin their work, they recognize the value of the orientation/training and have often written to tell us so. Following are some typical statements.

Pamela Karg wrote from Armenia, where she was a volunteer with the United Methodist Committee on Relief (UMCOR): "Without the wonderful weekend of preparation, I would have run into some frustrations. But you taught us well and I really did pay attention."

Barb Caldwell reflected on her experience as a volunteer in northern Chile after she had been there for six months:

> I never thought I would say this, but the workshop in Arkansas ended up being a pretty important part of my success here. I really took to heart the emphasis on recognizing and accepting cultural differences. I did refer to the culture-shock section two or three times when things were bad. It helped. Although, I am still in culture shock!

As a final word about the orientation/training, we will quote an affirmation of the November 2003 training weekend written by **Jean Houston**. She and her husband **Dan Houston** are the Iowa Conference UMVIM Coordinators. Jean wrote in their conference UMVIM newsletter:

> Last fall, Walt and Betty Whitehurst, individual volunteer coordinators, held a training session at Camp Wesley Woods for the North Central Jurisdiction. They invite the conference coordinators where the training is being held, so Dan and I had the opportunity to join the group. Several of these folks had traveled miles (all were from out of state—young and old and in between) to attend the training.
>
> I have to admit, with everything else going on, I was not prepared to sit in meetings from Friday evening through Sunday noon. *Wow*, what a weekend! I have sat through many training sessions at work and church, and this was the very best. Our *thanks* to Walt and Betty for their leadership and enthusiasm. I hope they will come back soon, and I invite each and every one of you to join in this wonderful training experience. If all of our United Methodist members had this training, we would have so many volunteers we wouldn't know where they could all be placed. Wouldn't that be wonderful—what a better world we would have today.

2

Individual Volunteers
and the Ways They Serve

There are varieties of gifts, but the same Spirit; and there are varieties
of services, but the same Lord; and there are varieties of activities, but
it is the same God who activates all of them in everyone.
—1 CORINTHIANS 12:4-6

*B*ecause the individual volunteer program is highly special-
ized, there are opportunities for many kinds of volunteers:
teachers, Christian educators, pastors, house parents and
helpers for children's homes and homes for older adults, librarians, office workers and computer experts, proposal writers, agricultural experts, health-care workers and hospital administrators, psychologists
and counselors, college and seminary professors and administrators,
coordinators for Volunteers In Mission and disaster response, persons
to do construction and repairs, and summer camp staff.

The list of opportunities for individual volunteers includes many
specific needs. In our work with individual volunteers, we found that
truly "the harvest is plentiful, but the laborers are few," and therefore
we were constantly obeying Jesus' command to "ask the Lord of the

harvest to send out laborers into his harvest" (Luke 10:2), since requests for volunteers always outnumber volunteers available to serve. It is a joy when exactly the right volunteer is found for a particular position. As coordinators, we felt it was our job to facilitate the process, but it was up to each volunteer to decide where and how to serve, after carefully considering the options and earnestly seeking God's guidance.

Pastoral Work and Faith Sharing

When Jesus met with the eleven disciples on the mountain in Galilee after his resurrection, he said to them,

> All authority in heaven and on earth has been given to me. Go therefore and make disciples of all nations, baptizing them in the name of the Father and of the Son and of the Holy Spirit, and teaching them to obey everything that I have commanded you. And remember, I am with you always, to the end of the age. (Matthew 28:18-20)

From that time forward, Jesus' disciples have sought to follow this commandment.

All individual volunteers are engaged in sharing their faith, sometimes through words of testimony and sometimes merely by their presence, since working in some countries will require nonverbal witnessing.

There are many whose major emphasis is pastoral work in some form, either as an ordained minister or as a layperson. The following are some examples of pastoral work and faith sharing by individual volunteers.

Sometimes a volunteer pastor can accomplish an amazing number of things in a short time. One example is Reverend **Robert Paulen**, a clergy member of the Baltimore-Washington Conference. Included in his final report after serving for two months in the Bahamas was the following list of tasks accomplished during his time there:

Maintained healthy congregational spirit and outstanding local leadership.

Completed plans for vacation Bible school this summer.

Held confirmation/membership classes. All wrote creeds and participated in the service of reception of new members.

Productive congregational board meeting with the conference president.

Well-received Wednesday night Lenten services and Bible study.

Initiated Maundy Thursday foot-washing service.

Held traditional Good Friday and Easter services.

Painted all exterior trim on manse and church.

Refurbished church exterior.

Purchased and installed new TV and VCR in Sunday school room.

Purchased and installed new water heater and shed for the manse.

Designed and ordered new church sign.

Approved drawing for remodeled chancel area.

Initiated clergy support plan for Wesley Methodist Church.

Reverend **Paul Perry** of the Southwest Texas Conference had a similar experience when he volunteered to serve as pastor of a church in Honduras for several months. He wrote:

Here I am in Utila. . . . Delightful place, and there is much need for pastoral presence and leadership. They have been without a pastor for more than three years. . . . There is such a shortage of pastors in The Methodist Church in the Caribbean and the Americas (MCCA). . . . No new clergy from this district since 1987! And the present pastors are really overworked.

I came in time to attend the district conference. What an experience! My first in seeing British Methodism at the circuit/district level at work. It was most beneficial for me to be here, and to better understand the larger issues.

Schools seem to be the major public face of the church here. There is a school in Utila, which has grades 1–12 and is restarting (after a twenty-year lapse) an evening GED program. . . . I have a chapel service for the students on Wednesdays at 7:00 a.m. in the church building.

Went to the outpost congregation Sunday morning on Utila Cay in a dugout canoe. Served Eucharist to the ten who came to worship, and then visited homes for home Communion.

Lay ministers also have made valuable contributions as volunteers. One of these was in response to the following request we received from Bishop Ruediger Minor of Russia in 1999 for a volunteer in St. Petersburg:

> Location: St. Petersburg
> Project name: Teaching English through the Bible
> Description of work volunteer will do: Work with youth and adults who are interested in learning the English language. Part of the students are members of the church; others have shown some interest in the Christian faith. The program will combine those interests by using the Bible as the major textbook and reading material for basic studies of the English language.

We listed the position, and **Don White** applied and was accepted. We first heard from Don after his arrival in St. Petersburg through a close friend of his in New Mexico, who wrote: "Don is basically shared by the St. Petersburg United Methodist pastors and spends different days with different pastors. This gives him a wonderful opportunity for experiencing a cross section of life in Russian ministries."

Later, Don e-mailed the following account of his teaching:

> Spent about two hours today speaking to one of my students about the fact that feeling she's "okay" isn't the criteria God uses for entry into his family. I felt a little frustrated because this person is beautiful, intelligent, and very kind to me, and has sat in these Bible classes for almost a year.

After completing subsequent assignments in Bethlehem and in El Salvador, Don went to southern Chile to volunteer at La Granja Agricultural School, where most of the students are Mapuche Indians. Although his major activity was teaching, he also enjoyed assisting with pastoral work in the nearby rural churches:

> Yesterday, Pastor Jorge Medina and I went to the *campo* (countryside) to visit some of his older church members who are either sick or

recovering—the first a lady with rheumatism and the second an eighty-one-year-old Indian fellow vibrantly alive now after being bedridden last year. It was a privilege to read Romans 8:11; James 5:13-15; and 3 John verse 2 to the lady. Pastor Jorge anointed her with oil, and of course God does any healing.

Martha Oldham, another lay pastor, went to Rwanda not long after the hostilities between Hutus and Tutsis had caused mass killings and unimaginable suffering. She worked with the United Methodist Committee on Relief (UMCOR), counseling women and girls who had been traumatized by the horrors they had endured. Many of them had been raped repeatedly. Husbands, sons, and neighbors had been killed.

In her book, *Africa: Lord, Hang Onto Me and Don't Let Go* (131), she describes her questions for God after being asked to work with these women and the reply:

> "Lord, what on earth am I, an American white woman, going to say to a group of women in Sodoma that will put your love in their hearts? I have never lost family in genocide. I've never lived in such poverty, and I have never faced AIDS up close and personal like they have. What will I say?"
>
> "Martha, you do your job and I will do Mine. What I want you to do is to love each of those women the way I love you."

College students have found effective ways of sharing their faith, even in situations where it is difficult to do so openly. **Tim Gates**, a college student from Pennsylvania who had visited Mongolia with a youth choir sponsored by the General Board of Global Ministries in the summer of 2001, spent the following summer as a volunteer in Mongolia, teaching English as a means of relating to people in order to witness for Christ. He wrote:

> Only two and a half weeks left for me in the land of Mongolia. It has been a wonderful time so far. Stretching and challenging for me,

49

to be sure. God has really done some neat things in at least me over the last few days....

I was hoping to give a testimony after the English class on Monday of this week, but things came up that made me think I should wait a day. There were only eight in class on Monday (many were still on holiday for *Naadam*—a big national holiday here). I prayed that God would bring many back for the next day so that most of the students (especially the regulars) would hear the gospel. God brought sixteen students the next day, perhaps the most there have ever been for one class!

I had the students talk about important people in their lives during the last part of class and then told them they could stay after class if they wanted to hear about who was most important in my life. I said, "Class is over, you may leave," but all stayed! This was a wonderful answer to prayer, and all were able to hear the gospel.

The next day I gave all of the students New Testaments in Mongolian. Many were appreciative. Please pray they read them. Just last night, I had a party at our apartment where we read the story of the lost son. Ten students came. We had biscuits and *tarag* (yogurt) to eat, and then read through the story. I had them act out the story and we then talked about the characteristics of the son and the father. Some of their answers were quite wonderful, and it was neat to see some of them really engaged in the conversation.

Beth Gossett, a college student from Texas who spent a summer volunteering in Laos, also wanted to share her faith while helping people in every way possible. She wrote:

I will be starting English classes with the church's youth group next week and classes with the village children the following week. I am so thankful that Christ shines brightest through my weakness. It's good to totally depend on him....

I wasn't able to really preach the gospel in the English classes at the village school, but I prayed for my students daily and thanked God for the opportunity to build relationships with them.... I was thankful to be able to teach songs like "Jesus Loves Me," "Seek Ye First," "Hallelujah . . . Praise Ye the Lord," and "This Is the Day That the Lord Has Made."...

God never fails to surprise me!... On the last day I was teaching, around fifteen students followed us home after school. I showed them my Bible and pictures from home, shared some English kids' books that I had brought, and invited them to come to church at the house on Sunday.

That Sunday (which was my last one there), around ten of my students came to church and stayed for lunch! I was *so* excited. It was amazing just to look out the window and see them flocking toward the church. At times I wondered how much of an impact I was making for the gospel, and to see those kids come to church was such an answered prayer.

Sometimes a volunteer's witness is to stand with the people in their struggle for peace with justice. Although all volunteers are working to bring about justice in one way or another, Reverend **Don Delaplain** and his wife, **Gloria Delaplain,** volunteers from the Southwest Texas Conference, went to Israel with the specific goal of showing solidarity with the Palestinians, while relating to Israelis as well in the spirit of Christian love.

Gloria wrote on the eve of their departure:

Don and I are leaving tomorrow for our long-planned-and-prayed-about Individual Volunteers In Mission service in the Holy Land. We'll be there for three months, serving most of the time in Ibillin, Israel, at Mar Elias Educational Institutions, founded by Melkite Catholic priest Abuna Elias Chacour, a Christian Palestinian and author of *Blood Brothers* and *We Belong to the Land.*

We'll also be spending part of the time in the occupied West Bank areas of Jerusalem, Bethlehem, Beit Sahour, and Beit Jala. We ask for your prayers as we stand in solidarity with the Palestinian people and work to bring peace with justice to *all* people in the land of our Lord.

Education and Christian Education

Individual volunteers are often asked to teach English, both in the classroom and in more informal settings. Some teach other subjects, and some are Christian education specialists. When assigned to schools or other mission institutions, volunteers are encouraged to relate to nearby churches, and most of them find this to be an enriching experience. They often help with church projects not directly related to their teaching assignments.

Mary Hedgcock, a Wisconsin deacon in full connection, went with her husband, **Frank Hedgcock**, a city planner and landscape architect, to work in Christian education in Bolivia while Frank helped Methodist schools assess their properties and begin long-range planning.

Mary wrote to her congregation in Wisconsin:

> Much of this week I prepared a curriculum workshop for the churches of the Montero area (three congregations).... I planned a demonstration lesson, made play dough, bought refreshments and crayons, copied handouts and worksheets, and sorted curriculum to give to participants.
>
> To my surprise, thirty-five Sunday school teachers, pastors, and district officers attended, representing nine different Methodist congregations. I had not understood the scope of the Montero area! All the participants walked or traveled by public transportation—many over an hour each way.
>
> As the workshop came to a close, I was reminded of Mark 8:1-9, the story of Jesus feeding the four thousand with seven loaves and a few fish. For four hours we had worked together learning to teach with the curriculum your donations purchased. All present were excited about returning to "feed" the children of their congregations.

Jim and Doris Long have provided a different kind of Christian education through marriage enrichment seminars, a ministry they began while they were missionaries in Mexico. They have continued to lead seminars in Arizona, where they live, and also in Mexico and Cuba. Having been to Cuba several times, and finding a great need for the marriage enrichment seminars, they began providing training to Cubans who can carry on the work there.

The Longs wrote after one of their visits:

During our three weeks in Cuba our work was in the further training of marriage enrichment facilitators in different parts of the island.... We had a three-day session with twelve marriage enrichment leader couples who had already led marriage enrichment events since our last visit two years ago. This was a very enriching time.

We had been requested to guide a program on sexuality and sex in marriage, with two major emphases: to teach the leaders, and to prepare them to teach others. We learned much about the Cuban reality and how the Bible and Christian concepts need to be applied, in the churches especially, and hopefully extend out into the society as a whole.

Volunteer English teachers are requested in many countries, giving the volunteers an opportunity to interact with people in both church-related and secular settings. **Tom Hyle,** a retired NASA engineer and teacher from Texas, and his wife, **Nancy**, a writer and poet, had planned to teach English with the Amity Program in China in the summer of 2003, but that year's summer program was canceled due to an outbreak of SARS (Severe Acute Respiratory Syndrome).

Tom was able to go the following summer, and he wrote:

Just wanted to say hello and let you know that I am teaching English in Nanchong, China (Sichuan Province). This is the third of a four-week summer English program through Amity Foundation....

The students are middle-school teachers and are very bright and warm people. We each have a class of about twenty students and teach four and five classes each day. We prepare at other times. It is a very rewarding experience.

We do not preach but show our faith through our teaching and interaction with our students. We have attended Chinese church services four times, and these are moving even though we don't understand the words.

Mary Osif, a college student from central Pennsylvania studying in New York City, took a semester off to teach English in Poland. She published her musings on the Internet in the form of a blog, which made for interesting reading as she posted her day-by-day experiences and feelings. For example: "What did Mary learn today? Further knowledge that Polish high schoolers are the same as American: they aren't interested in the Civil War, either. . . . I think, more than anything, none of them understood what the point was of learning about the American Civil War."

Experienced teachers can be useful in helping with teacher education. **Carolyn "Cally" Curtis** (daughter of Tom and Margaret Curtis, director and associate director of the Southeastern Jurisdiction's UMVIM program for nineteen years) wrote from Belize about her assigned task of developing workshops for teachers, in addition to teaching high school art classes and leading the Art Club:

> The most time-consuming task I've been given is to develop workshops for primary school teachers, a program that demonstrates how to integrate the Belizean arts-and-crafts syllabus with core curriculum subjects: math, language arts, geography, history, social studies, and natural science.
>
> That means I've been studying the many cultures of Belize (Kriol, Garifuna, Maya, Mestizo, Mopan, Mennonite, Rasta, Spanish, East Indian, and Asian), as well as their food, folklore, art, music, flora, fauna, and history. To make the projects affordable, I have been gathering as many recyclable products and natural materials as I can, along with various craft supplies that come in large quantities at a cheap, cheap price.

Volunteers often find that they learn from their students. **Staci Martin**, teaching in South Africa, reported:

> Ronald is a student of mine and one of my favorite teachers. He is the only male student in my computer class. He is a black South African twenty-something with impeccable patience. Intelligent. Strong. He gives me grief about my Americanese and my wackiness, but I seem to never lose my patience with him.
>
> We learn by our mistakes. It's taken about seven months of teaching my nine students for them to learn that it is okay to make mistakes. No one is going to hit them. No one is going to yell at them. No one is going to degrade them. At least, not in my class.

Ronald joined the group a couple of months ago. He makes mistakes. He learns from those mistakes. One thing that is unique about this student is that he is willing to try. Fail. Succeed. He tries and doesn't give up.

And I suppose this is the thread that is woven in this country, South Africa, that I find so appealing, so beautiful, so deliberate. No matter what color your skin is, there is hope and resilience. Perseverance. A need . . . need to try.

Library Work

Volunteers have served in libraries both in the United States and in other countries. We will illustrate how valuable their service can be with the story of **Morris and Ann Taber**. During their two five-month periods of service in Zimbabwe, Morris taught history at Africa University and Ann started a library for the primary school. A newspaper article describing the library opening referred to "Ann Taber, the American philanthropist." Morris's comment was, "I never thought I'd be married to a philanthropist."

Soon after they began their work in Zimbabwe, they reported:

Ann has begun her work at Hartzell Primary School. She has found the headmaster congenial and welcoming, appreciative and thoughtfully concerned about how best to help his children learn—including how best to use Ann's skills and whether such materials as we can get would really be useful. He appears very dedicated to giving them the best education possible with resources at hand.

The library-to-be has to have a leaking roof and ceiling fixed, it must be termite-proofed and painted, and shelves must be built before Ann can set it up. . . . Meanwhile, she is working in the staff "tea room." She is settling in well, though is a bit heartsick at seeing a school trying to teach with almost no books in the classrooms. . . .

Later they added:

Ann's work here continues to bear fruit. Much of her success is due to the active support of the school staff. They put together an elaborate weeklong reading emphasis program with posters, poems, storytellers, and time out for reading. In one activity, children went out into the community to solicit donations in order to buy professional books to put in the library for the teachers. The teachers, students, and community are getting involved and have ownership in this endeavor. The room that will be the library is almost completed.

During their second time of volunteering in Zimbabwe, there was more good news about the Hartzell school library:

The exciting news concerns Mr. Maramba's dream of building a new three-room library. The school's PTA decided last summer that the current library was overcrowded and began plans to build a bigger one. They have already gathered about a third of the cost and need only another $10,000 U.S. for the building itself.

While some of us were discussing possible means of raising the money, a Volunteers In Mission team arrived from Michigan at the end of January. One team member, a newly retired engineer from Midland, became so enthusiastic about the project that he is arranging for his home church to raise the money. Although there are some important steps still remaining, the gathering of estimates and the hiring of a contractor are under way....

With a large area for stacks and another as a reading room, Ann will also soon be back in the position of encouraging people to collect and send more books.... As a result of the ever-widening circle of sharing, a school with no library in January 1999 should have a well-stocked, three-room library building by late 2000!

Later they wrote about the library's completion:

The library, painted in bright lemon, stands out distinctively among the other white-painted classrooms. Its trained librarian and her assistant have entered data for the entire 8,900-book inventory into a donated computer and will soon begin computerized checkouts. Twenty months ago there was no library at all!

Office Work and Computers

Volunteers with office and computer skills have helped in mission settings in many parts of the world, including the United States, and many of them have taken time off from their work to do so.

Danita Nelson, a volunteer from Alaska, provided much-needed office help at the NOMADS office in Trotwood, Ohio. She wrote:

> I am settled in Trotwood at the "hospitality house" provided by Cross Point Church. I have been busy at the NOMADS office for the last several weeks (lots of phone calls and mailings as we match NOMADS requests with the projects for the winter/spring periods). I am learning lots, and hope that I'm being helpful.

Later, Danita was able to be equally helpful in her next assignment at Crossroads Urban Ministry in Dallas, Texas.

Dan Shelly reported from Kenya Methodist University, where he worked in the computer lab, and his wife, **Nona**, helped computerize the library:

> We spent the second week here at Kenya Methodist University, working in the computer lab as well as the library. I managed to get the two servers we brought with us up and running and networked with several of their lab machines, a *major* challenge based on what we had to work with.
>
> Nona managed to get the library card catalog moved into an Access 2.0 database on an old machine running Windows 3.1. They have 3,500 books cataloged, but since the hard drive only holds 40 megabytes, they will soon run out of space. The university is growing about 100 percent per year and expects to move into new facilities when they are completed in April or May this year.

Medical Work

Medical professionals, in spite of their busy schedules, often find ways to volunteer their services in places where medical attention is lacking.

Carolyn Pesheck, who worked for a major pharmaceutical company, went to Maua Methodist Hospital in Kenya to assist in the pharmacy department. While there she was also able to visit the newly organized School of Nursing at Kenya Methodist University:

> On Tuesday afternoon of this week, I went to Kenya Methodist University in Meru (about fifty kilometers away, one and a half hours by car) with a woman who works here a few days a month in the Disabled Community Center. She also teaches at the university and is helping to set up a degree program in nursing. . . .
>
> Kenya Methodist University has only been in existence for about eight years and is the only university in this province of Kenya. At this point, there are about eight hundred students, about half of whom are "distance learners," meaning they come and pick up the course syllabus (borrowing what books they can from the library) and take it home to try to learn the material, coming back only a few times during the semester, then try to pass the final exam. . . .
>
> The campus has three large buildings: the library plus classrooms and offices, the administration building plus classrooms and offices, and a very large chapel. It also has a slew of smaller buildings, one of which has a classroom/lab for sciences. This one classroom covers all courses that are taught in both biology and chemistry. . . .
>
> The degrees offered at the university are limited—the only science-based degree is applied biology, although science is also taken by some of those getting secondary-school teaching degrees. Science courses will also be taken by the nursing students when they start, including chemistry, biochemistry, biology, and anatomy. If and when students start a medical degree, more courses will be needed.

Judith Richerzhagen, a nurse from Shoreline, Washington, volunteered at Kenya Methodist University and while there had an opportunity to visit Maua Methodist Hospital:

> What a week! I was at Maua Methodist Hospital for five days. How intense it is to be immersed in the culture away from many of my coping techniques. Part of the challenge is in seeing how hard the Kenyans have to work just to live. Women wash clothes by hand in cold water after carrying the water. Drying the clothes is a challenge—you only

have the daytime, as it rains much of the night. Humidity is 80 percent plus, so things don't get dry anyway. Milk and drinking water need to be boiled before using. Everything has to be cooked from scratch. . . . Some things that are available are too costly. Bread is a cheap staple. . . . Oh, yes, then there is all the medical equipment they don't have. This hospital does have mosquito nets, and there was only one patient per bed while I was there. Imagine washing sheets for a two-hundred-bed hospital and hanging them on the line to dry in 80 percent humidity. Most of the sheets are paper thin.

Some medical students have been allowed to do their required practicum under the supervision of physicians in other countries, where their help is much appreciated. **Alyssa Wenger** and **Misty Williams**, medical students from Arkansas, went to La Ceibita, Honduras. Alyssa wrote:

Misty Williams and I worked in a clinic in La Ceibita seeing or treating at least thirty patients a day, Monday through Friday. . . . Although we would have liked to have been able to stay longer, we treated over three hundred patients and provided around 130 pairs of eyeglasses to people who really needed them. Of course there were many chronic problems we were not able to address, such as hypertension, but we feel great about those people with acute illnesses whom we were able to treat successfully and help educate.

We were really nervous about the idea of working in a clinic by ourselves treating patients and were quite overwhelmed with the number of people surrounding the clinic every morning just waiting to see the "doctoras" that they had heard about. . . . Our work supervisor was Dr. Iván Mejía. We actually lived with him and his family in Tocoa, Honduras, and he helped us to get organized and have access to antibiotics during our time in La Ceibita.

The only other colleague we had was a nurse who was in La Ceibita a couple of days with us. She was there our first day and was instrumental in helping us learn drug dosages of antibiotics that came in powder form, something we'd never had to deal with before. She also instructed us on treating parasites, a task we have never come across in Arkansas. . . . We have greatly improved in our medical Spanish and have enjoyed some wonderful Honduran foods and beverages.

Retired physicians and nurses can serve for longer periods of time. **Sharon Romich**, a professor of nursing, served twice as a volunteer with the United Mission to Nepal (UMN). During her first year there, she worked for nine months in Kathmandu, teaching at the Lalitpur Nursing Campus and overseeing clinical experience with the students at Patan Hospital. Then she went to a district capital, Tansen, to work at UMN's new nursing school and at Tansen Hospital. In 2001 she went back to Tansen to teach pediatric nursing for three months.

Sharon wrote during her first time in Nepal:

I am enjoying starting to work at Lalitpur Nursing Campus. I really like the nursing faculty and think teaching at their level will not be a challenge, but teaching at their level in Nepali will be the challenge. . . . Everyone, including the Nepali and the expatriates, is very supportive and helpful. I have been warmly received, with a much more gentle landing than I expected. . . .

The students have started their clinical experience at Patan Hospital, and I am getting my first look inside the Nepali health-care system. The patients are so sick. Many of their conditions are routinely treated without difficulty in the United States. For instance, tuberculosis is a big problem here. People live crowded into very close, unventilated homes and use a fire inside for cooking. Many of the people are poorly nourished, so the TB bug passes easily in these conditions. . . .

Death is an ever-present reality in the pediatrics ward. . . . We had a very sick little two-year-old admitted yesterday with pneumonia. This admission was into a ward with eight young children in open beds and cribs, whose parents usually slept on cots under the beds.

The staff worked with this sick baby for a couple of hours, but were not able to reverse his overwhelming pulmonary problems. He died, his body was removed, and within an hour there was another equally sick baby in that crib. All this took place in full view of the other parents and little patients. . . .

One little girl, age two, went to surgery for a skin graft of a burn she suffered last week. How do you imagine they take children to the operating room in Patan? Well, her parents weren't there when she went to surgery, so her eight-year-old brother was in charge of her that day.

When it was time for the girl to go to the operating theatre, as it is called here, her brother just picked her up and trotted up the stairs and into the operating room with her. Children, actually all patients, must have a family member present at Patan. The families do most of what we would call nursing care. So when Mom or Dad can't be there, they send an older sibling.

Dr. **John Clarke**, a retired surgeon from Virginia Beach, Virginia, agreed to go to Kenya so that a surgeon from Maua Methodist Hospital could take a much-needed study leave. He wrote of his experiences there:

I have now been at Maua Methodist Hospital for nearly three weeks. As in any new situation, initially almost every task was difficult. By now, I have gotten to know many people on the hospital staff and have found them to be a wonderful, Christian group and very desirous of being my friends. I now am able to call many of the nurses, operating room staff, clinic staff, administrative staff, kitchen staff, carpenters, and especially the information technology staff, by first names. Knowing the information technology staff is especially important, since I have to go to their office and plug into a phone line to send e-mail. . . .

The staff, from the physicians to the groundskeepers, are dedicated Christians who live their Christian commitment every day. They consider their work here at this hospital a service mandated by and for their Lord and Savior. They treat the patients with great kindness and compassion and with real skill, considering the limitation of supplies, equipment, and facilities.

Every morning, seven days a week, starts with a 7:30 a.m. chapel service. The night crew who are going off attend chapel, as do all the day crew, including all of the physicians. There usually are about one hundred people present. The service is led by a member of the staff and includes a capella singing, scripture reading, prayer, and a brief meditation. The service generally lasts about twenty to twenty-five minutes. The services are a wonderful way to begin every day. . . .

Immediately after chapel, the physicians meet and have morning report. I then go to the surgical wards, where I have morning rounds with the nursing staff and see my forty or so surgical patients.

At least one volunteer decided to stay long enough to establish a significant medical ministry. In 2001, Dr. **Phil Plunk**, a dentist, went to Guatemala to set up a comprehensive health-care ministry, which he described as follows:

> The name of our ministry, *Salud y Paz*, translates as "health and peace," appropriate for a country that has just seen the end to thirty years of civil war—a war in which the indigenous Mayans whom we will be working with endured efforts by the government to exterminate them....
>
> *Salud y Paz* was formed to bring medical and dental care to a hurting people in need, and to stand as a symbol of peace, saying to people who have been told for centuries they do not count, that indeed they do count. In fact, they are so loved and so important that people from a far land will change their lives and come to them in the name of God....
>
> The *Salud y Paz* logo is a triangle of physical health, spiritual health, and emotional health. Physical health needs are readily seen. Spiritual health is found in one's relationship with God and must be nurtured and fed. Emotional health, a feeling of happiness and contentment, is less readily apparent sometimes. However, without a balance of all three there cannot be true health.
>
> Notice that in the center of the triangle is the Cross, because even with the "three healths," our lives are incomplete without God in the center.... Only with the balance of health, plus God in our lives, will we find true peace....
>
> The most important news is that we opened the clinics this week. Fifty patients a day each were seen by the doctor and dentist.... There were a lot more than that lined up. Oh, the need is so great! The clinic is the central meeting place of twenty-six surrounding communities. The *bomberos* (fire fighters) keep telling us that each village has one thousand to fifteen hundred people. Go ahead—do the math yourself....

At the end of 2001, Phil reported:

> We closed out the year of 2001 having seen 2,871 patients in the clinics, not bad for having them open only six months in total. Analyzing our budget, we provided services at a cost of less than $18 per

visit, including all the medications dispensed. While that is not bad, we hope to cut that amount in half this year, since we will not have some of the major expenses of setting up and installing the equipment, import taxes, and repair of the vehicles.

In June 2008, Phil wrote:

We now have five clinics in operation, with a Guatemalan staff of twenty-four people. We and our volunteer teams provide approximately forty thousand patient visits a year. We have four surgery teams at Camanchaj per year doing general, facial, GYN, and eye surgery. We are opening a preschool in January 2009 and will eventually have up to eighty children in that program.

Working with Children

Whether in orphanages, day care, preschool programs, or elsewhere, working with children is one of the tasks to which God has called many persons who apply to serve as individual volunteers. The work they do varies, but all have in common a love of children and a desire to give them a chance for a better life, as shown in each of the following examples.

Sandy Entenman, after volunteering in Kupres, Bosnia, went to work in the *Hogar de Amor y Protección al Niño* (Home for Love and Protection of the Child) in Colima, Mexico. She wrote:

These people have six orphanages, a retreat center, and a men's and a women's house, and they are building an administration office. This complex where I now live has five buildings, each for a different age-group. All this is supported by a local church and by many churches in the United States and in Canada.

Some names you will read frequently in my correspondence are Robert and Carmen, who are responsible for volunteers. Robert came in 1989 to help after an earthquake, met Carmen, and never left. They married, took in three children, and by the next year had nine—and now up to one hundred in these buildings.

I have been assigned laundry detail for the downstairs where I live. I do this in the morning before ten o'clock. At that time I tutor a student named Andi and help with his homework. I have been given this task because Andi has ADD (attention deficit disorder). I try to keep him on task for a half hour, then I move upstairs to teach English to the eleven- to fourteen-year-old girls.

We have another group of students (girls) in my house at five o'clock. These will be the girls I will get to know the best. Their stories (which I am only beginning to know) are horrendous: every type of abuse and mistreatment. Two of the girls are especially interested in English because they will soon be adopted by people from Michigan.

Nicole Windhurst, whose volunteer service in Zimbabwe included being instrumental in providing family-style houses for the children, to replace the large, aging building where all the children stayed together, wrote eloquently about her time there:

I arrive at the orphanage at eight each morning when bath time begins. This is a chaotic assembly-line process where one woman washes and I am supposed to dry and dress. She is hopelessly faster than I am, so there are usually many naked wet bodies running around.... The clean clothes are piled on the floor where I sift for something remotely close to the child's size that doesn't have too many holes in it. Clothes I slapped on a three-year-old yesterday will be on a seven-year-old today and an infant tomorrow. This process was difficult for me to swallow at first, but I now see the necessity for it when resources are so scarce....

The rains have come and brought a wonderful, exciting time to Zimbabwe.... Last night I was playing with the children, and in storybook fashion, the skies got dark, thunder echoed, and lights struggled to stay with us—all activity was suspended in time as thirty little pairs of eyes stood motionless, looking at me and waiting for instruction.

Before I could open my mouth to direct the children under the veranda, the skies parted and we screamed and squealed our way out of the downpour. We flopped in a muddy dog pile onto the half-dry concrete, giggling and smearing wet hands on one another's faces.

I looked back into the courtyard to make sure that all the little ones were with us, and what I saw moved me to tears. Pauline, a tiny three-year-old girl, was spinning and dancing in the rain—laughing hysterically and singing *"Mvura, Mvura"* (rain, rain) to her own funny tune. In three months this girl has changed beyond belief or recognition, and to see her dancing, singing, and most of all smiling, was one of the most touching moments I have known. . . .

My first day at the mission, the matron gave me a tour of the hospital, orphanage, and maternity wings. Babies that are abandoned at less than nine to eleven months of age (before they can sit up, eat porridge, sleep most of the night) are put in the maternity wing and cared for by a twenty-four-hour nurse.

This is where I first met Pauline, slumped over in an awkward position and eyes staring at no one and nothing in particular. When we walked in, she reached for my hand and the blanket fell off her. It was one of those moments when I had to consciously stop myself from jumping back or gasping aloud. She was insanely tiny—her arms were literally no thicker than wooden school rulers, eyes sunken in and hair falling out all over the place.

I calmly took her hand and asked how old she was, thinking she must be somewhere between six and eight months by her size. When the matron told me she had just turned three, it hit me like a ton of bricks. As I took back my hand and we began to walk away, little Pauline began crying and then howling. The matron saw the pained wince on my face and patted my shoulder. She said, "The first few months are always the hardest for them. After that, they learn not to expect so much."

The next week Pauline was transferred over to our wing with the rest of the big children. She was refusing to walk or move, and at times would not even sit up. She never spoke to anyone, but cried nearly the entire day, sometimes screaming *"Ambuya, ambuya, uya pano! Ndiri pano!"* (Grandma, Grandma, come here! I am here!) It was heartwrenching to watch. I was determined to see her get well, so I fed and bathed her whenever I could, and held her on my hip as I walked around. . . .

Seeing her now, she is thin but healthy, hair growing thick, not only walking but dancing in the rain. More than her physical appearance is the light in her eyes—the dull, glazed-over, lifeless look has been replaced by this light, this joy that you cannot help but smile at. . . .

Later, Nicole wrote about another touching experience she had:

One warm day in February I only had a few minutes for lunch, so I grabbed a hunk of bread and cheese and headed up to the orphanage where I knew the kids were expecting me. Now, I have long ago learned that there are two ways to bring food to the kids—you either have forty pieces or you have none (or you prepare for serious trouble!). Knowing this, I worked fervently to stuff my chipmunk cheeks before I rounded the bend in the footpath.

I was, of course, instantly spotted by one of my favorite little girls, Lyvia, who is seven years old and too cute for words. After a ceremonious bear-hug greeting, there was no hiding my little treats. I broke the chunk of cheese in two, gave her one and popped the other in my mouth. She looked curiously at the mysterious white blob, looked back at me, and promptly ran away. I was shocked—I thought, "Well, there's gratitude for you!"

I followed her up the path and found her hiding behind a three-foot cement half wall protecting her prize from the other hungry mouths. I slid behind the wall unseen as one of the staff women came by carrying bundles of laundry. She saw the little girl hiding and suspiciously asked, "Hey—what are you eating?"

"Um... don't know..."

"What? What do you mean you don't know? Why do you put a thing in your mouth that you don't know?"

"I just don't know.... Niko gave it to me."

The woman smiled and saw me on the other side of the wall listening. She teasingly asked, "Hmmm... What if Niko gave you a *snake*?!"

Lyvia looked indignant and said, "Niko not give me a snake! Niko loves me!" At this point, I faded behind the wall, unnoticed, with tears in my eyes.

After Nicole returned home, a fellow volunteer in Zimbabwe, **Gil Gilman**, wrote about Nicole's work:

Last April we finally moved the Fairfield kids into their new homes. This was the dream of Nicole Windhurst [who had returned to the United States after completing her volunteer assignment], and in April it finally became a reality.

The difference I saw in the children absolutely amazed me. Once they were out of that big, institutional-style building with a dozen "mothers" and into individual homes with one twenty-four-hour mother and six or eight "siblings," they became instant families. Each mother takes great pride in her family, and the competition between houses is having fantastic results. The kids are cleaner, better dressed, and just downright happier.

About a week after they moved into their new homes I was at Cecillia Thobani's house. She is the assistant administrator. I occasionally drop in on Cecillia first thing in the morning because she makes a fine breakfast! On this particular morning there was a knock on the door and a little one was standing there saying, "Mommy wants to borrow a broom."

The fact that the kids were referring to their house mother as "Mommy" brought tears to my eyes. I went home and sent an e-mail to Nicole Windhurst to tell her about this wonderful little incident. It took a lot of people, a lot of work, and a lot of money to get these twelve homes built, but once Nicole made up her mind what was needed, no force on earth could have stopped the project.

I had met Cecillia Thobani, a Zimbabwean who had just graduated from teachers college, about the same time that Nicole arrived here. I introduced the two, and that one little act may have been the most important thing I have ever done here!

Community Development and Agricultural Work

Working with the community, whether urban or rural, can be an important contribution of volunteers. Following are some examples of this aspect of volunteer work.

Julie Meyer helped the Tsimane people become registered with the Bolivian government as an official indigenous group, enabling them to apply for government programs that had not been available to them before. She described the process in a series of reports:

January 4, 2001—Today I got a small taste of what lies ahead because I entered the Tsimane territory.... In my enthusiasm, I thought, "Oh, it can't be that far!" I was dead wrong. My guides were Lisardo and Carmelo, two younger Tsimanes. . . . When they told me two hours, it seemed like no problem. What I wasn't prepared for was the pace. People say the Tsimanes walk fast—but little idea did I have of how fast they actually walk! Carmelo went first with the rifle (in case of tigers), then Lisardo and then me. They walked so fast I literally couldn't keep up and every few minutes had to jog to close up the widening gap. . . . It must have been a pretty funny sight: the two of them walking calmly along with a *gringa* (North American) trailing behind with her fancy clothes and boots.

January 25, 2001—I went to the INRA [land reform agency] office this morning to look for the Tsimanes' documents, since I've looked everywhere else. . . . I ended up at the Catholic Church's office for indigenous affairs talking to an extremely articulate lawyer/pastor. . . . They deal with land in smaller pieces (not reserves), which is exactly what we have. He showed me seven titles that they just got, absolutely amazing for this part of Bolivia. He also told me that they have been wanting to work in my area, but have no contact. Now, February 10 he is flying out to do a land workshop with all the Tsimanes. My job is to gather them all, which means a lot of walking in these next few days!

February 14, 2001—Saturday night the lawyer arrived along with his assistant. . . . By nine the next morning, we started the meeting to discuss land issues. Six Tsimane communities came: Bajo Colorado, 10 de Junio, Aguas Negras, Chocolotal, Santa Rosita, and Tacuaral. The largest community is Tacuaral with sixty-three families. At one point, I counted more than one hundred people!

The meeting took forever, since everything was translated into Tsimane. Four of the communities already have the documents that legally establish them as an indigenous community. Two others have no papers, which means as far as the government is concerned, they don't exist.

I was extremely impressed with the lawyer. He explained the process clearly and encouraged questions. The communities had to formally decide if they wanted the support of the office, and all six communities agreed. . . . They drafted a formal letter asking for support, and it was all signed and complete by ten thirty that night. . . .

At the end of the day, the Tsimanes presented both Dr. Filemon and Inocencio (his assistant) with a beautiful set of bow and arrows. Each set had different sizes, for hunting all types of animals. Everyone felt encouraged and hopeful that this was the beginning of finally getting a title for their land. I'm now convinced that land is the first step for these communities to improve their living conditions, and to maintain their culture that is quickly disappearing.

March 15, 2001—My involvement with the process is mostly one of communication between the communities and Filemon with the Catholic Church in Trinidad. It is the communities who are organizing and starting the long process of legalizing on paper their title to the land where they and their families have lived for hundreds of years. . . . I feel honored to be allowed to participate and witness this small movement in an isolated part of Bolivia. Since I represent The Methodist Church here, I have also thought a lot about the church's role in situations of injustice. For me, it is no accident that the legal support is coming from the Catholic Church. As Christians, we have an obligation to stand with the oppressed, be it farmworkers in Oregon or Tsimanes in Bolivia. I have had the privilege of observing and working with people here who live a life committed to their faith.

April 16, 2001—Since it was Holy Week, we only had classes until Thursday. . . . We still had to get the Tsimanes' land documents signed, so Erasmo and I decided to use Friday to enter a community called Aguas Negras. Neither of us had ever been there, but we figured it couldn't be that far. We were wrong! We left at nine on our bikes and finally arrived at one in the afternoon. The last part didn't even allow bikes, so we left them on the path and continued on foot. . . .

Since this community doesn't have any documents, we had to write their "Founding Act." No one can read or write, so Erasmo and I dictated the document and read it back to them. Signing is done with thumbprints. I don't have a stamp pad, so I brought a big black permanent marker to color their thumbs. . . .

While Erasmo and I were in Aguas Negras, Lisardo (a Tsimane from Río Colorado) hiked into Diez de Junio to sign their documents. . . . We finally finished all six communities, and the next day I traveled to San Borja to leave the signed documents at the Catholic Church. Although it is only the first step, it is in the right direction.

June 6, 2001—Right now, I'm waiting for three Tsimanes to arrive for a quick meeting. Tomorrow they are traveling to La Paz to present their land demand for six separate communities. The lawyer is going to meet them on Wednesday in La Paz in the main office of INRA. The indigenous community sent me two hundred *bolivianos* (Bolivian currency) to cover their transportation, and they are going to pay for their own food. Andrés is going to have them at his house so they don't have to pay for a hotel. This is an important step in the process, and we are very excited. The communities still have a long way to go, but at least they are moving forward.

Jim Gulley, a volunteer in Cambodia who was later commissioned as a missionary, assisted Cambodian Methodist pastors and congregations with various kinds of community and agricultural development:

> Nearly every congregation aspires to have one to four hectare farms to produce for a "rice bank" from which the poor may take "loans-in-kind" during the three hungry months (March–May). Loans are paid back in-kind at the rate of 1.2 bags for each bag of borrowed rice. Interest sound high? Comparison with the two bags charged by typical "rice lenders" puts the interest rate in perspective....
>
> Wells have been dug providing clean drinking water to villagers. Training on pig production has enabled farmers to be more successful and to "pass on the gift" of an offspring to others. Small loans have provided capital to generate jobs and income, including weaving, rice noodle making, and loans to support watermelon, mushroom, and fish farming, among others....
>
> Similar village-level projects will be supported in other locations under the Agricultural Development in Rural Cambodia (ADRC) project supported by the Finnish Methodist Church. One of our partners, the Center for Livestock and Agriculture Production Integrated, will introduce pig-biogas-vegetable production in one of our villages....
>
> Under the ADRC project, four Regional Agriculture Committees, including experienced agriculturalists, have begun to oversee development, implementation, and monitoring of new projects. My central task has been to train and support the Cambodian United Methodist Church leaders to take on these roles.... Working in Cambodia is truly a process of "walking together" in mission.

Community development takes place in the United States as well, sometimes with the help of volunteers from other countries. **Ana María López**, from Bolivia, wrote about her work with the Latino community in northern Virginia:

We have begun a support group for women, called *Conversaciones y Cafecito con Cristo* (Conversation and Coffee with Christ).... The purpose is to reach the Hispanic community, get to know Hispanic/Latina women in the neighborhood, talk about subjects of interest to women, listen to talks by visitors representing community and government agencies, nonprofit organizations, and religious leaders.

We try to find speakers who are Hispanics, but if necessary we can provide translation. We have already had a talk about child development and some of the characteristic behaviors at each stage of a child's life. Then the floor was open for comments, questions, and sharing of life experiences.... We provide child care, and distribute reading material for spiritual growth and other matters of interest to the community.

United Methodist Committee on Relief

The Mission Volunteers office works closely with the United Methodist Committee on Relief (UMCOR) when volunteers are needed to work with UMCOR projects around the world. UMCOR volunteers, unlike most individual volunteers, work in secular settings where they are involved in humanitarian projects, working with non-Christian communities. Their witness may be nonverbal, and they may not have access to local Christian congregations with which to share in worship and fellowship.

The "Guidelines for Volunteers In Mission Teams Serving in UMCOR Non-Governmental Organization Settings," published in October 2000, includes the following statement about volunteers who work with UMCOR, which applies to individual volunteers as well as team members:

United Methodist Volunteers In Mission is a servant ministry. Volunteers serve under and with local leadership. As servants, volunteers focus on the needs of others. They do not put first their own convenience, their accustomed ways, their needs. They try to understand and respect the people and the culture they serve. When volunteers serve the poor, they often change their own perspectives and priorities.

71

Hal and Margaret Waters are among the volunteers who have served at the UMCOR Sager Brown depot in Baldwin, Louisiana. They described their work there as follows:

We began 1999 in Louisiana as we began 1998. This time we were in Baldwin at UMCOR Sager Brown with NOMADS. Some of the NOMADS worked in the community repairing a home for an invalid woman and her family. Others were painting and repairing buildings at the center. The rest were working in the UMCOR Depot.

Sager Brown began as an orphanage for black children following the Civil War. It developed into a school over the years. The land for the school was purchased by Ms. Sager and Ms. Brown and given to the Women's Division.

It was closed in 1978 and was unused until 1992. Hurricane Andrew struck, and UMCOR was heavily involved in relief following that disaster. Finding a great need for a place to store supplies, Sager Brown was reopened. UMCOR has refurbished it and in 1996 dedicated a depot larger than two football fields where donated emergency supplies and equipment are received, sorted, and redistributed (hence the name depot rather than warehouse). Inside are sorting tables and multitiered storage racks that are serviced by front-end loaders.

The facility is staffed almost entirely by volunteers, and they are always looking for more. Housing and food services are available on advance arrangement with the volunteer coordinator.

During 1998, shipments from UMCOR Sager Brown totaled 230 tons. Barely past the midpoint of January 1999, large amounts of relief material have been arriving since Hurricane Mitch pummeled several countries in Central America.

NOMADS and other volunteers were busy preparing food and health kits, along with bottled water, for Honduras and Nicaragua, and two seventeen-ton shipments were sent out. The supplies have been collected by church members across the nation.

Emergency food boxes for North Korea and 750,000 seed packets sorted by volunteers and placed into family-size packets of ten in a sandwich-size ziplock bag were included in the fifty-two-ton shipment. Another project was the sorting and packing of garden seeds for shipment to the Dominican Republic to assist in hurricane recovery there. Some nineteen thousand packets of seeds were donated and sent to the depot.

Yasmine Rana was able to help children and youth begin to overcome the effects of trauma suffered during the war in Bosnia:

The Sarajevo Youth House was established by UMCOR in December 1995. Since 1997, it has been registered as a local nongovernmental organization. The Youth House provides local, returning, and refugee children ages three and up with educational, psychosocial, and recreational support in a safe and nurturing environment, enabling them to rebuild their communities and their lives. Self-expression is encouraged through classes in music and art. Programs are also offered in languages, computers, and media. There is also a successful preschool playroom program.

One of the strongest statements of creative expression is from the Youth House's photography program. Through this program, children were given tools to capture images of Sarajevo toward the end of and after the war. Many of these photos have been sold to benefit the Youth House. They are chilling images of the people and buildings that experienced destruction. What was particularly powerful about the photographs was their perspective. Behind the lenses were children who were witnesses to what was happening to themselves and to their city.

To volunteer in the Youth House is to listen to personal accounts of the past and to see the future. Adolescents and teenagers shared with me their experiences of the war. Through fables used to teach language, children identify with the characters that "lost" something or someone. The art classes began to replace the greenery that was cut down during the war with a makeshift forest made from paints and paper, so the younger children would be surrounded by trees.

The Youth House employees and volunteers strive to create a setting for children to recapture what was stagnated and lost. Despite the conditions of the House, which would mirror the conditions of any postwar social service facility lacking funds and supplies, many children from the community are members.

Construction and Repairs

Volunteers can provide a much-needed service by overseeing construction projects or by being available for maintenance and repair of church properties. Some volunteers have found that using their construction and maintenance skills is a rewarding way of serving others, as the following reports indicate.

Paul Letot of Nepal observed:

> United Mission to Nepal has one hundred flats [homes] to maintain plus the headquarters to keep repaired. I have done building, light electrical, some bricklaying, and a little carpentry. I try to stay out of their way and be helpful when called on....
>
> I am also taking language lessons. I go with local people when possible. I have great accommodations here at the guest house. I do a lot of walking and have been to two picnics. I'm eating well and feeling fine.

Don and Constance Waddell were charged with overseeing repairs to a Methodist camp in Chile. Constance wrote:

> Don has been busy repairing the damage . . . a septic system that ran on top of the ground . . . an electric system that was dangerous, and the one still unsolved—no water. We buy the water and have it put in the two tanks. We are searching for the illusive *noria* (pump) that the contractor assured everyone was there.
>
> Churches in Chile have helped . . . an industrial-size stove and a large oven were given . . . chairs and beds supplied, and lots of blankets. Our church in Rogers, Arkansas, has supplied funds that have done huge amounts of work. Also family and friends have given gifts, and then we have tapped into our own funds. Don is working overtime to try to help the Chilean church take responsibility. . . . They are thrilled to have the camp open, and small carloads come by as they visit the beach and bring bread and cheese to share with us at *Once* (afternoon tea).

Not long afterward, Constance wrote again:

> Great news that the Chilean Methodists are taking more responsibility for the camp. This weekend we had a group of fifty-six from a Santiago church, and during their family weekend they also washed windows and worked on chopping weeds under cottages. Week before

last we had twenty who spent the night and did the new benches of cypress logs at *Monte Sinaí* (Mount Sinai) outdoor chapel.... Next weekend we have forty coming, and they will paint our neighbors' house. It is a terrible eyesore, made up of leftovers from original cabins—but also we pray it is a boost to them as they try to make do.... The same weekend we have a camp of one hundred.... They know we will not have enough beds and that the electricity will probably go out several times, but they still want to come....

Don and I are thrilled to see so much accomplished in so short a time. The new multipurpose building is a great incentive to get folk here. So we have told the committee and Bishop Grandón that we will leave by the first of May. Don's health doesn't get better, even though he is extremely happy and would like to stay here forever. The hours drain both of us. We *love* what is happening here, but by the end of the busy season, we will be ready to go.

Hosting Volunteer Teams

Some individual volunteers are asked to take on the responsibility of hosting Volunteers In Mission teams. They are a liaison between the visiting teams and the host community, and may also serve as translators in places where a language other than English is spoken. It is demanding work, but often rewarding because of the relationships that are formed and the work that is accomplished.

Reverend **José Pulgar**, a retired pastor from Chile volunteering in Bolivia, wrote about his work with an Oklahoma UMVIM team:

We worked at a place called Khonani, then in Cala Cala and later in Katavi, near Oruro, at eight hundred meters higher than La Paz, on the Altiplano (the "rooftop of the world"). The team saw 542 patients, and the construction of a chapel progressed quite a bit. We had three doctors, four nurses, two educators who worked with the children, an accountant (who took care of the group's finances), two builders and with me three, since I worked with the group.

I created a revolution, since a brother from the church and I, in two days, shoveled three and a half tons of gravel, added sand to the mix, and laid bricks. (My blood pressure rose, and the doctors gave me medicine, which I am still using.) A marvelous experience! (It's better to die from hard work than from laziness.)

When we went to Cala Cala, an Aymara nurse told us that she used a megaphone when she was going to give vaccinations to call the people, but that she had forgotten to bring it. And she asked if someone who could yell loudly would climb up a hill and call the people, but it had to be done in Aymara.

Since the majority were from Gringoland, I, always the busybody, offered to do it. And so I asked the nurse to tell me the words in Aymara and I would repeat them. So we went up the hill and I began to shout at the top of my lungs what she said: "Doctors have come, those who are sick come quickly," "We will take care of you with love," "Come . . . sick people, come."

I shouted in Aymara however it came out, without knowing what I was saying, and apparently they understood me, because in fifteen minutes they began arriving, and at twelve thirty when we had to return to Khonani (eight kilometers from Cala Cala), they kept on coming. I was about ready to ask the nurse to tell me how to say in Aymara "Stop coming and go back home, sick people."

Paul and Janet Burger spent a summer in northern Mexico facilitating the many work teams that go there each summer through the Hands Together Ministry. They wrote:

The week of May 26 began a very busy summer of mission teams building small concrete homes in Río Bravo. That first week we had five teams building eleven houses. The summer will continue, receiving an average of four to five teams per week.

It is a hectic and busy time. The families receiving homes live in poor wooden structures with dirt floors. Each team that builds a house helps get a needy family into a small but decent home. The teams also pay for the cost of the materials and a *maestro* (brickmason) for each house, which is $1,400. Families are selected through an application process set up through DIF (social service agency of Mexico). They are visited by a DIF coordinator, Paul, and the head mason, to determine if the family is in need to receive a house. Sometimes a family has to wait a long time to actually receive the home.

Mini medical teams come every other weekend to provide health care for those in need. People here suffer from diabetes, high blood pressure, and various aches and pains. Many do not receive any other care because they cannot afford it. Some teams bring an eye doctor or dentist. Nearly 170 people were seen each day at the last clinic held. Waiting begins early in the morning before the clinic opens. Each person is given a number. When the numbers are called they are signed in and then wait to be seen first by nurses doing triage (blood pressure, pulse, and blood test if needed, etc.) and then by the doctor. Some patients may have to wait most of the day to see a doctor.

At the end of the summer, Paul and Janet summarized the work accomplished by the volunteer teams:

We have built 105 houses this summer with the aid of about 1,400 volunteers. We have dramatically changed the lives of these 105 families in two ways, through building their new houses and getting them out of their dirt-floor shacks; and spiritually, as the teams shared the gospel and God's love with them.

Chuck Wheat recruits volunteer teams for Costa Rica by informing them of the benefits of having an experienced coordinator to receive the work teams:

Every project is fully scouted, with detailed cost projections and all necessary permits.

Teams need bring no tools or supplies, with the exception of a limited list of items, principally electrical items, which I do ask teams to purchase and for which they are given credit against their construction fund contribution.

All arrangements are made for in-country transport, lodging, and food at very reasonable costs.

Care is taken to promote team interaction with the local congregation in work, worship, and fellowship. Vacation Bible school is treated as a "must do" activity.

A "local excursion" menu is arranged in the vicinity of each site for a break during the time at the job site. The last day before leaving the country is reserved for a *paseo* (excursion trip), with a menu available for a number of options out of Alajuela.

While on-site, the team's work leader is "in charge." While either David Elizondo or an equally competent local professional will be on-site to give guidance and keep the wheels from falling off, we want the team to feel that it is *their* mission.

I meet each team at the airport and accompany them to the site, leaving only when necessary to obtain supplies, for medical emergencies, or to go get the next team. David and I do not participate in team devotionals or other activities, again to promote the special bonding that is such a precious feature of the Volunteers In Mission experience.

Safety and security are a high priority for us. A plan is developed for each project site for medical and other emergencies. I have two vehicles in Costa Rica, of which one is always on-site in case of need for an emergency evacuation.

A great failing of many VIM missions is the lack of feedback to answer the question: "And then what happened?" Through my newsletter and website, I try to fill that void.

Unexpected Duties

Although volunteers are given a job description before they leave home, most learn upon their arrival that they are expected to do many things not mentioned in their official invitation.

Barbara Tripp, director of the Marion Edwards Recovery Center Initiatives (MERCI) in Goldsboro, North Carolina, described how a brand-new volunteer, **Diane Walrath**, was able to provide an unexpected service as soon as she arrived at MERCI:

Diane arrived safe and sound even if early. You might be happy to know also that she earned her keep on day one. We had an accident (our first!) when one of the youth got hit on the face with a hammer (long story), but Diane was close by and knew exactly what to do and how to do it!

The youth was back out today with no more than a slight cut visible, no stitches needed. Diane has also jumped right in and taken on the task of organizing the tool area and setting up a checkout system.

Good start, huh?

A volunteer who went to Zimbabwe to work with children at Fairfield Children's Home had an unexpected opportunity to serve at Africa University. She was provided with an apartment on the university campus, which enabled her to be involved in evening prayer services with some of the students, and her apartment became a place where the students could come to talk, play games, share their stories, and pray together. Because the apartment had a kitchen with a stove and refrigerator, the volunteer invited students for meals and was given African cooking lessons in return. She felt like she was a mother figure for at least a hundred students who were far from their homes for two to four years and, like her, were living in a culture other than their own.

Gil Gilman wrote about what a difference another volunteer made in her two months in Zimbabwe:

> I didn't spend nearly as much time with her as I would have liked because of the needs of my own projects here, but what I saw in her is what Individual Volunteers is all about. The talent she brought to Zimbabwe is what the Greeks of two thousand years ago called "agape"— unconditional love and fellowship within the Christian community.
>
> I was invited to a little party on the eve of her return to the United States. It was a love fest. She made a difference, not by coming to Zimbabwe with great plans and projects, but with the faith that God would show her the way and let her make a difference. She has touched the lives of more than one hundred students, fifty orphans, and countless others in a way that she never could have dreamed before she took that first little step in faith.

3

Volunteers in Cross-cultural Situations

You can't stay in your corner of the Forest waiting for others to come to you. You have to go to them sometimes.
—WINNIE THE POOH, IN *POOH'S LITTLE INSTRUCTION BOOK,*
BY A. A. MILNE (E. P. DUTTON, 1995)

Culture Shock and Cultural Adaptation

*C*ulture shock, or culture stress, is the disorientation one feels when adjusting to a new and different environment. It can happen anywhere, even within one's own country. For someone from the suburbs or from a rural area, going into the inner city is like going into a developing country. For a city dweller, the lifestyle in a rural area may be equally disconcerting.

One volunteer from Alabama who had served as a short-term missionary in Los Angeles and as a mission intern in the Philippines told us that she found more cultural differences between her small town in Alabama and the city of Los Angeles than between her town and the town where she served overseas.

Some symptoms of culture shock are homesickness, depression, sleeplessness or excessive sleeping, chemical use (prescription drugs, alcohol, etc.), irritability, boredom, hostility toward nationals, inability to work effectively, problems with personal relationships (marital, family, friends), overeating or loss of appetite, headaches, and psychosomatic illnesses.

Persons experiencing culture shock are usually in denial, and until they realize what is happening to them it is unlikely they will get beyond the stage of irritability or hostility. Some will become angry and strike out at things they do not understand; others will withdraw and are in danger of clinical depression unless they work at getting beyond their culture shock.

Volunteers are told in their orientation/training that the more they educate themselves about culture shock, the better they will be able to deal with it. Before beginning a mission venture, volunteers should learn as much as they can about the culture they will encounter: values, traits, characteristics, and lifestyle. Ways this can be done include reading as widely as possible, talking with international students and other persons from the place where they are going, seeing movies from that country, and beginning to learn the language if they do not already know it.

Almost everyone in a new cultural setting experiences, to a greater or lesser degree, several distinct stages of culture shock. There are different ways of describing these stages, but all are similar. The description we prefer to use is from L. Robert Kohls's *Survival Kit for Overseas Living* (4th ed. [Yarmouth, Maine: Intercultural Press, 2001], 97).

As we received communications from individual volunteers, it was often easy to discern which stage of culture shock they were experiencing by the tone and content of their messages. Below are some examples that illustrate the stages of culture shock.

Stage 1: Initial Euphoria

The first stage of culture shock is the "honeymoon period" when we are fascinated with the many new and different things we are experiencing.

Nicole Windhurst wrote the following greeting from Zimbabwe:

Hello everyone, and greetings from the beautiful country of Zimbabwe! This place is absolutely amazing—I have been here for ten days and it feels like I have been a part of this community all my life. . . . This region is gorgeous, the people are incredibly friendly, my apartment is fabulous, and the orphanage is both wonderful and heartbreaking.

Kera Leutung wrote from Bolivia:

Juan Carlos (my Bolivian friend from the plane) went back to the States, and Diane (another U.S. volunteer here at the church) has been traveling all week, so that has left me to fend for myself and it has been great! It has forced me to learn my way around and practice my language skills solo. I had dinner with the missionary family here last night, who analyzed my attitude as being in the "honeymoon" phase, where everything is new and exciting and I don't want to go home.

Stage 2: Irritability and Hostility

The second stage of culture shock, irritability and hostility, begins when we realize that almost everything in the new culture is different and strange. We feel isolated and uncomfortable, and tend to reject all that is unfamiliar.

After almost a year in Zimbabwe, **Nicole Windhurst** wrote:

Last Sunday (December 30), I finally found some free time and all the necessary ingredients to make my favorite family tradition, white roll-out Christmas cookies. After weeks of searching, I had finally found a tiny bottle of vanilla extract and then even managed to finagle eggs on a Sunday (when everything is closed here). Sugar has been rationed lately, but I decided that the Christmas tradition was worth the whole cup needed. I mixed some margarine with the elusive vanilla, finagled eggs and scarce sugar, and was *loving* the way my kitchen smelled.

I opened the sealed Tupperware flour container and, to my dismay, found a tiny black bug munching away at my final major ingredient.

Now, I hate bugs passionately, but I was not to be deterred. I spooned him out and kept on measuring. When I spotted the second and third, I realized that some serious courage and sifting were both in order. Lacking a formal sifter, I began to slowly improvise with a pair of forks and a stiff upper lip.

Forty-five minutes, eight bugs, and two hand blisters later, I came across a one-inch lump that just wouldn't sift, so I pitched it in the sink. As the water dissolved the flour, I saw it—a silky slinky mass with thousands of tiny white maggots running for dry land. Mouth open and eyes bulging, I slowly turned to my bowl of painstakingly sifted flour and realized that it too was full of the nasty little creatures. I had been so focused on the obvious black bugs that I had totally missed the tiny babies squirming around.

Since I had already mixed half of the "clean" flour into my precious batter, everything was simply ruined. It was almost too much to take—this was not part of the family tradition. I held back the tears as I threw two kilograms of flour and my beloved, yummy-smelling dough in a sink of hot water.

Staci Martin wrote after her first month in South Africa:

It was last week when I began the journey in search of a *USA Today*. I went to five different stores, five different days.... Each time, each salesperson attempted to sell me something else. My patience wavered when all I wanted was a *USA Today*, *not* a *UK*, not a *Star* (South African paper), not a European paper. I wanted an American newspaper—a paper that was written by Americans, in American ink, on American paper, about American news.

On the sixth day, I arrived at Exclusive Bookstore where they had a *USA Today*. It was the only one left. I looked through it and only the front section and sports section were included. An incomplete newspaper. I asked them if they had any in the back. The salesperson remarked, "No."

I said, "Why are you selling an incomplete paper? I am not willing to pay full price." She was taken aback a little and said, "All right, 10 rands (US$1.25) instead of 22 rands (US$2.50)." As I paid, I noticed that the *USA Today* I was about to buy was a Wednesday paper—five days old. And so it goes...

Stage 3: Gradual Adjustment

Stage three of culture shock, gradual adjustment, is when we learn, little by little, to decipher foreign behavior and customs. For some volunteers, it seems to come naturally.

Bob May, four days after his arrival in the Philippines, wrote: "Immediately got a haircut. I showed up here with pretty long hair and I could tell it made a poor impression, so on day two I cut it."

For most volunteers, however, the adjustment process takes longer.

Cally Curtis wrote from Belize: "It's taking me time to adjust to the new, which presents itself at every turn.... It's like I have to seep into their rhythm, to learn and appreciate their ways and systems, before I can dovetail my own ideas with theirs."

Cheryl Lafferty said about her work in Chile:

> *No one* will ever understand the energy it takes to form sentences in another language unless you have been in the same situation. Sometimes it takes me five days to write a note to the parents: one day to start writing, one day that I can't look at it again or think about it, one day for someone to read and correct it, one day for me to make the corrections, one day for me to get it printed and copied. I'm used to being able to write, read, and talk on the phone at the same time at my old job.

Stage 4: Adaptation or Biculturalism

Stage four of culture shock, adaptation or biculturalism, is when we have come to accept and enjoy the foreign culture, and integrate our way of life into it, without losing our appreciation for and enjoyment of our own culture.

Kera Leutung wrote from Bolivia:

> I think I came with the North American attitude of working for immediate results, and I have finally realized that "making a difference" can also be done with the simple gift of presence. (Also, nothing moves that quickly here.) They have been living without me, will

continue to once I go, and I will most likely be the one who is significantly impacted.

Greg Pimlott, who spent time in the Democratic Republic of the Congo, wrote the following:

> It was a successful term as far as learning how to live in Congo. I am slowly learning French (and, even more slowly, learning Swahili), and I have gotten used to taking every Saturday morning to hand-wash my laundry and do other necessary housekeeping.
>
> I am beginning to get to know more people in the community (Congolese and expatriate) and am really getting the hang of this living in a different country thing. Even as I get more and more comfortable in this new environment, it still is not home, and I will always be, in many people's eyes and even in my own mind, someone who doesn't exactly belong here.

Facing Frustrations

Although most volunteers learn to adapt to a new and unfamiliar culture, there are inevitably frustrations that challenge even the most dedicated and determined volunteers. Contributing factors may include not knowing the language well, uncomfortable or even dangerous conditions, unrealistic expectations on the part of the volunteer or on the part of those receiving the volunteer, perceived indifference of persons with whom the volunteer is living and working, financial problems, lack of knowledge of the laws—written or unwritten—in the place where the volunteer has been assigned, and conflicts within the church or community.

Volunteers usually take frustrations in stride, especially those who are able to reach out and find persons who provide help and support. The ones who fare best are those who are willing to work under local supervisors, adapt to the local culture, be observant and ask questions, listen to the persons with whom they are working and not impose their own will, and have a servant attitude without allowing themselves to be used.

The greatest help in overcoming frustration is a healthy sense of humor, which is very much in evidence in some volunteers' reports about the frustrations they have faced.

Jeanie Pennington wrote from the Czech Republic:

> I went with Pastor Botos (Pavel) and a student, David, to downtown Prague to go to an English bookstore.... I tried to exchange a bill at two different places, but neither place would take it. The bill had an edge that was not straight and there was a small hole in the bill. (The bill came from an American bank!) Anyway, I guess I will have to bring this bill home with me.
>
> We ate at the Chinese restaurant. When the bill was presented, I gave the waitress (a Chinese who speaks Czech) my credit card. They accept credit cards at this restaurant, but the man who knows how to use the credit card machine was not there. I had to pay cash! The bill was 529 Kc (Czech crowns). That is a little over $24. I only had 500 Kc! I thought I was going to have to wash dishes! We scrounged our coins together. I had $24, and Pavel added the rest! Whew!

Frank and Mary Hedgcock wrote of their experiences in Bolivia:

> March 1, 2001—When we returned to Montero last weekend we found four boxes of Sunday school curriculum waiting for us (mailed November 3)! They went by ship to Santiago, Chile, up the western slope of the Andes mountains to La Paz, and down the eastern slope to Santa Cruz and Montero. They were a bit damp from humidity, but now are all quite fine.

Later in the year, the Hedgcocks wrote:

> Everything takes longer here! Preparing meals, finding a shower curtain, purifying drinking water, drying laundry on humid days, traveling from one community to another, preparing lesson plans and translating them into Spanish. . . . Clean water is not generally available. Lack of concern for sanitation disturbs me. Unrefrigerated meat

hangs in the market, bags of household trash are pitched over the fence or dropped by the walk at the *Colegio Metodista* (Methodist School) where we live, and an old water heater rusts away in our yard.

Sharon Romich wrote after one of her frustrating experiences in Nepal: *"Ke game?* (What to do?). For those of you who are new to 'Notes from Nepal'—it is a favorite Nepali phrase used for all the things that don't go according to plan here."

Sharon's words reminded us that when we arrived in Temuco, Chile, as missionaries, we were invited to dinner by five North American nuns who gave us a lot of good advice, including their observation that whenever anything goes wrong, all you have to do is raise your hands in the air and say *"Qué le vamos a hacer?"* (What can we do about it?). We found that this phrase worked beautifully in almost every difficult situation.

After hearing the phrase from Nepal, we began looking for it in other cultures and languages, and have come up with the following list of similar expressions used throughout the world:

- Japanese Americans: *Shikata ganai.* (It cannot be helped.)—Japanese American State Senator Takasuki, California, quoted in *The Greatest Generation* by Tom Brokaw (Random House, 1998).
- Inuit: *Ajurnamat.* (Can't be helped.)—Jeri Bishop, missionary in Alaska.
- Swahili: *Akuna matata.* (No problem.)—Irene Mparutsa, Zimbabwe (volunteer in Cambodia).
- Democratic Republic of the Congo: *Imana* (Swahili for "fate")—Dr. Michael Sluss, individual volunteer.
- Khmer: *Ort panya'ha.* (No problem.)—Irene Mparutsa.
- French: *C'est la vie.* (That's life.)—Dominique Gettliffe, French volunteer in Democratic Republic of the Congo.
- Jamaica: *No problem, mon.*—Carl and Margaret Ennis, who served in Jamaica with the Ecumenical Institute.

- U.S.A. (youth slang): *Whatever.*—Members of the Individual Volunteer Orientation/Training group in Dulac, Louisiana, February 2004.
- Australia: *No worries, love.*—Shannon Williamson Gallo, Virginia Beach, in a column in the *Virginian-Pilot*, Norfolk, Virginia, Tuesday, February 17, 2004.

Learning the Language

One of the most difficult tasks facing many volunteers is learning the language of the country where they serve, and yet it is essential to learn as much of it as possible. Language is a vital part of any culture; and to really understand a culture, it is necessary to have some idea of how the language is structured. "I wish I had known more of the language" is a statement we have heard many times from volunteers.

We have suggested to volunteers who do not already know the language that they attend a language school for at least a month of intensive study, and we recommend that all volunteers who need to learn a second language begin studying before they go, using books, tapes or CDs, or online lessons. Once they arrive in their place of service, they are likely to be so immersed in their work that it will be almost impossible to learn the language unless they have a foundation to build on.

Following are some thoughts on language study that volunteers have shared with us.

Nicole Windhurst commented on learning a new language in Zimbabwe:

> In my nine months here I have been making a fairly serious effort at learning Shona, which is a beautiful language spoken by about 85 percent of the people in Zimbabwe. I have heard it said (by someone famous, I'm sure) that to be fluent in a language is to be fluent in a culture. I think our American schools make a grave mistake teaching only Spanish, French, German, and other European languages to our

children. The child that knows Chinese, Arabic, Swahili, or Hindi doesn't just know a language, but also understands another perspective on life.

Learning Shona not only teaches me enough vocabulary so I don't get laughed at in public, but also teaches me the Shona perspective on those words and the way they fit into life here. Water and rain are the same word (*mvura*) because there is no water without rain, all water is "rainwater." Drought and hunger are also the same word (*nzara*); there is no hunger without drought in a farming society. To hold someone (*bata*) and to help someone (*batsira*) are related words—that is how we help. Spirit (*mwari*) and friend (*shamwari*) are related words—a friend is a kindred spirit. Forgiveness (*rusunguru*) and freedom (*rusunguku*) are almost identical words in Shona and may be a lot more closely related than the English language gives them credit for.

Sarah Smith, a volunteer in Peru, sent a thoughtful analysis about language learning:

A priest who was a fellow student at the *Instituto* (language school) commented to me that the only type of poverty North Americans really have is linguistic poverty. When students from the *Instituto* leave to go to work and serve in a new part of the world, they encounter poverty that they have never previously experienced. Coming from wealthy countries like the United States, it is impossible to fit into this poverty. Missionaries are often stereotyped as wealthy, and this is one of the many things that sets them apart in their new community.

The only poverty that North Americans come with is linguistic poverty. We stumble over words, we make no sense, and we show ourselves to be poor in a different sense. We are usually gently corrected, and everyone may have a laugh at the same time. By correcting us and serving as role models for pronunciation, our new friends see that they can help us. They become our tools to opening the door to a new culture.

Living Arrangements

One of the challenges in making a volunteer placement is to determine where the volunteer will live. Living arrangements vary greatly, from a room in a private home to a fully furnished house. The most extreme arrangement we know of, which we learned about only after the volunteer's return, was a sofa bed in the parsonage living room. However, most volunteers have adequate lodgings, although they may lack some of the comforts of home, as seen in the following descriptions.

Rob and Pam Porter wrote from Ghana: "The greatest difference between this trip and the Angola trip two years ago was the immersion into the local Ghanaian culture. This time we were expected to live separately, by our own devices; pump and filter the water, buy groceries, fix meals, etc., as local (fairly affluent) Sunyani residents."

Reverend **Paul Perry** reported from Honduras:

> The mission house/manse is very comfortable. It has a fully stocked kitchen, microwave, TV, refrigerator, washer (no dryer), fans, and even air-conditioning. It is located about fifty feet from the water, and you can hear the waves lapping up the shore from the back bedroom. Private bath for the master bedroom, and two other large bedrooms for groups who may be here as Volunteers In Mission. Grocery store next door. Only downside: the sand flies have had a field day with "new meat" in the person of Paul F. Perry! Guess I've been duly inaugurated.

Some volunteers live with families, or share a home with others. The following descriptions are typical of the experiences of volunteers who live with a family or in a group setting.

Julie Meyer wrote from Bolivia:

> I absolutely love my house. It has one big room with a couch and tables, a kitchen, shower, and two bedrooms. One bedroom doesn't have anything in it, though. It's really the lap of luxury, since it is bigger than all of the other teachers' houses. I even have hot showers! It's great. I heat water on the stove and pour it into a pail in my shower. There's a rope attached with a pulley, so up it goes, and it mixes with the colder water....
>
> Recently, I've gone from living alone to two roommates. One is Misi ("cat" in Quechua and Tsimane), a kitten that the missionary in

91

San Borja gave me. He's only about three months old and very playful. The good news is I haven't seen any mice since he arrived.

My other new roommate is Irma, Estela's youngest sister from
Guatemala. She's visiting Estela [a missionary in Río Colorado] until
August, and since I had the empty bedroom, I thought it would be fun
to have some company. She's nineteen and very calm and sweet. She
also wears the traditional Guatemalan dress, and it's beautiful.

Jeanie Pennington reported from the Czech Republic:

The family with whom I am living is very poor financially. He used
to be in the information technology field where he was doing well financially. When he was called to the ministry, his income changed to
one-fourth of what it was! As I said, they are poor financially but are
rich in spirit!

Pavel's apartment is arranged as follows: when you open the door,
there is a hallway. In that hallway, there are several closed doors. The
doors lead to the restroom, the living room, the bedroom, and the bathroom. From the living room, one can go into the kitchen. I must leave
their area and go to my room adjacent to theirs.

When I open my door, there is a small anteroom with another door
leading into my room. My room has a portable sink, a table with a
computer on it, a bed, several pieces of furniture I use for clothing,
and another table. I believe we will be using my room for the English
lessons.

Their church is in the same building in which they live. We only
have to go down a flight of stairs, across a short area, and up another
flight of stairs.

Culinary Adventures

Adapting to a new kind of diet is something that may require time
and effort, since the food offered to volunteers may be different from
what they are used to. Mealtimes, and the number of meals per day,
may also be different.

Mary Osif wrote from Poland:

We had kielbasa and potato salad with yummy tomatoes for supper.
By the way, Adam gave me the rundown of Polish meals in the car, and
I wonder if Tolkien's Hobbits were really based on Poles. First breakfast, second breakfast, lunch, dinner, and supper. Maybe I'll just start
having elevensies and afternoon tea to fill in the gap.

For someone accustomed to a wide variety of menus, having the
same foods at every meal, day after day, may quickly become boring.

Steve Paylor, volunteering in Chile, commented: "Breakfast is at
the cafeteria, usually the ubiquitous rolls—nearly all of the *pan*
(bread) in Chile is the same sort of flat roll—with hot milk or coffee.
Both beverages take a while to drink because of waiting for them to
cool."

On the other hand, a "meat and potatoes" person may find a daunt-
ing array of foods, many of them highly spiced, and not know how to
deal with it. Except for general guidelines for maintaining good
health—water that is boiled or chemically treated, no ice, no un-
cooked vegetables or fruits that cannot be peeled—we recommend
that volunteers obey the commandment Jesus gave his disciples when
he sent them on a mission: "Eat what is set before you" (Luke 10:8).
The basic diet in most countries is nutritionally balanced, and if the
people there survive on it, so will their guests.

Julie Meyer wrote from Bolivia: "You'll be interested to
know...that I can eat an entire plate of rice and beans and—if not
love it—enjoy it!"

Stephanie Saunders said of her eating experiences in Chile: "I
thank God because I have had no trouble with the food or water here.
Last Sunday after enjoying (key word) a plate of cow intestines, blood
roll, and various other parts that I will not mention, I could only praise
God for giving me the stomach of a missionary!"

Increasingly one finds North American–style restaurants even in
remote places, but unless they are places where the volunteer's friends
and colleagues can afford to eat, it is better to refrain from what might
appear to be a self-indulgent luxury best left to the tourists.

Cheryl Lafferty, also in Chile, said: "Howard lost the bet with his sister that there were no McDonald's here in Iquique. Sad to say, but there are actually two! Sorry, Howie, you owe your sister Donna $5!"

Purchasing food is an adventure in a new cultural environment. Dr. **John Clarke** wrote from Kenya:

> Despite the small selection of food in the store, I have eaten extremely well. There are many fresh fruits of every variety that you can think of, and they all grow locally. I have just fixed a salad in a large bowl to use for several days, and it contained the following: oranges, bananas, grapefruits, pineapples, passion fruit, and mangoes, all fresh.

Bob May discovered new varieties of food in the Philippines: "The ketchup here is sweet, and it's made from bananas. They put it on a lot of things—like fried chicken. All things requiring tomato sauce are made from this banana ketchup. Spaghetti sauce is really banana ketchup sauce."

Frank and Mary Hedgcock described one of Mary's cooking ventures in Bolivia:

> Last Saturday afternoon Mary baked bread with the women of *Cristo Obreros* (Workers for Christ) church. While the outdoor oven was heating, several women mixed four kilos of rice flour, two kilos of mashed *yuca* (a starchy root), a kilo of melted pig lard, two kilos of grated goat cheese, and several cups of water with salt and sugar in solution. After thoroughly kneading the dough, we all shaped the dough into little rings and placed them on greased metal sheets. They baked in about fifteen minutes in a very hot oven.

Nicole Windhurst had some creative eating adventures due to food shortages in Zimbabwe:

> I have just finished my gourmet dinner—fried egg on white toast with orange Kool-Aid. There may not be any chefs banging on my door for recipes, but I am grateful for every meal I cook and every bite I eat.

Two weeks ago the government sanctioned price controls on basic commodities, which is great for the average consumer, but takes the manufacturers a bit to adjust to. We'll have three or four days with no bread but tons of margarine, then no oil but tons of sugar, no laundry soap and too much bread . . . and so on.

I always have enough to eat, but sometimes the combinations get straight-up weird—favorites have been peanut butter on stewed cabbage, baked beans on toast, or papaya sandwiches. The stranger the food gets, the deeper my appreciation grows, and I gain an acute insight into how truly God provides.

Many individual volunteers have learned that trying new foods (and drinks) can be an interesting experience.

Sharon Romich wrote from Nepal:

I went to 7:30 a.m. Mass with Sister Pat and Sister Bernie (Maryknolls). . . . After service, they fed us breakfast: chickpea *tarkari* (vegetable stew) and big fluffy pancakes that reminded me of Ethiopian bread. The debate on the way home was whether we also had tea or coffee. It was very hard to tell. They said it was coffee, but mostly it was milk and sugar. . . .

I have bitten the bullet and told Didi that I will drink *biscie* milk (buffalo milk) this time; she is pleased, as Nepalis think it is so much better than powdered milk. So she gets me some fresh and then boils it to pasteurize it for me. One thing for sure, it has a healthy or unhealthy amount of cream. And the cream is very thick and clingy just like *biscie* fat.

Julie Meyer, while volunteering in Bolivia, told of her experience with a new drink:

I recently tried some *chicha* (a drink) at a birthday party and it was actually pretty good. I asked them how they made it and they told me it was a mixture of corn and *yuca* (a starchy root). The next day, when I went to the water pump, Concepción was busy grinding up some corn (with a large stone) to make another pot. Curious, I went over and greeted her. She calmly leaned over and spit a mouthful of corn she was chewing into a pot before answering me! To speed the fermentation, she and Ascencio were chewing all of the corn first! So, now I know how they made the *chicha* I tried the day before!

Adjusting to the Weather

At a meeting of the directors of the Mission Volunteers program of the General Board of Global Ministries, **Ana María López** had been invited to share her experiences as an individual volunteer. She began by saying, "I came from Bolivia to Virginia in January. In Bolivia, that is summer. It was so cold in Virginia. It was very hard to get used to. In Bolivia, the weather is so"—she paused, searching for the right word—"so *normal!*"

Ana María's words reminded us of some of the things other volunteers had written us about the climate in the places where they were serving.

A volunteer from New Hampshire, used to a cold New England climate, said: "Hot begins my Vietnam story. Not Africa hot, as I used to think the gauge. Surface of Venus hot is closer to the mark. Humid too. As humid as it can get. I like it."

Volunteers from Florida, accustomed to a warm Southern climate, commented: "No one told us how cold it would be in Nepal—and there is no heat in the houses."

A volunteer in Korea wrote: "We have finished the hottest summer I have ever spent in my life, which followed the coldest winter I had ever lived through."

Daily Life

Volunteers have the opportunity to depart from their normal daily routines and experience new lifestyles. It can be frustrating or exhilarating, boring or adventurous, lonely or constantly surrounded by people, or all of these at once. It is almost certain to be memorable, as the following excerpts demonstrate.

Sandy Rowland wrote about her observations while living in Bosnia:

Riding down the mountain each morning we pass the same things, but each day I see something different. Saja drives like an Indy 500 race-car driver, and I have held on to the door handle for dear life many times, missing cows, dogs, cars, and big yellow buses that are the public transportation, and they travel on the little mountain roads at high speed. She says I can drive, but I decline.

The other day we passed a little lady. Saja knows everyone, so we stopped to say hi! She was old and bent over, carrying a bundle of sticks tied to her back. As I looked into her face I saw many years of hard work and wrinkles. The sticks were tied tight with rope, and I wondered how she breathed. I asked if I could take her picture. She declined, and I respected that. Although I won't have her picture on paper, I will have it forever in my mind. She was a returning refugee. Frail and delicate, I wondered how she survived. . . .

If you come to Bosnia you will have to: deposit your shoes outside the door (I have been caught wearing shoes and given little slippers to wear inside); like cabbage, sour cream, cow's milk; like to walk; drink lots of coffee, work in the garden, and wear clothes for about four or five days at a time, no air-conditioning, and have people drop in at your house anytime of day or night and not be upset.

Bo Fagin wrote about team loyalty in Senegal:

Yesterday Senegal lost the championship game of the African Cup of Nations to the Camaroons, 3-2, in penalty kicks. The country is in mourning. I was coming home on a bus just before the match started, and the streets were about empty. Many small shops and stalls were closed. Everybody was at home watching the match on TV. . . .

In the States most of the serious sports fans are men. Not so here. It is an equal opportunity sport. I was at a marriage on Saturday and was seated in a circle of women who were having a very serious and animated conversation in Wolof, a language I do not understand well. I had sort of spaced out until I realized that every second word was Senegal-Cameroon and that these were *serious* football [soccer] fans.

When it was all over, it was the wife, where I am staying, who cried. . . . In a country too smart to get into wars, the national football team carries the pride of the country on its shoulders.... As a long-suffering Chicago Cubs fan, I am teaching them the ultimate expression of hope, "Just wait until next year."

New Styles of Worship

Volunteers may encounter worship services that are very different from those they are accustomed to. Worship can be more formal or much less formal, even charismatic or pentecostal. Still, it is important for volunteers to be a part of a local congregation whenever that is possible, even if they do not understand what is being said and sung. The Holy Spirit can touch our hearts whether we comprehend with our minds, and worshiping in a different style and language and cultural setting can be an enriching experience.

In addition to worshiping in a local church, volunteers sometimes find worship services in English, and attending services in a familiar language can provide much-needed spiritual refreshment.

Other volunteers face the challenge of working in a secular setting, or in a culture ruled by a religion other than Christianity, where no organized Christian worship is possible. They learn to rely on their own spiritual resources, and on communications with Christian friends by mail or on the Internet. Some have even found Internet church services that provide a virtual worship experience—not as satisfying as being in a real church with real people, but an acceptable substitute when nothing else is available.

The following are descriptions of worship experiences that volunteers have found noteworthy.

Mary Osif wrote from Poland:

> I have to say that church was kind of funny today. The sanctuary is basically the only room, and it's probably a little bit bigger than my living room and dining room at home. Maybe one and a half times the size. So, it's small. Plus, there's no carpeting really, so you can hear basically every sound. And half the men were coughing here and there. And it's chilly, so everyone's wearing their jackets. Plus, there were

two babies who were sooo talkative. And one, maybe both, of them kept getting away from their parents and running around. . . .

I spent most of the service biting my lip to keep from laughing. Yeah, talkative babies can be annoying, but honestly, what toddler really understands what's going on? There's a reason everyone always comments on how quiet a baby is in church. And during the sermon, one of the toddlers got away and ran right up behind Kris and then right back to his mom. So, yeah, church was noisy today.

Bob May wrote of his worship experiences in the Philippines:

I have only attended United Methodist services here. All of them have been in Tagalog, but most of the churches also have English services. My neighbor preaches at a different church each Sunday, and he has taken me with him. The services are pretty much the same as the ones we have back home, with the following exceptions:

I was amazed by the continuous buzz of the congregation. There were always people talking during the service. I suppose it was mostly the children, but there are a lot of them in the crowd. The church is packed with children.

Communion was taken first by the men, then by the women, then by the youth, and finally by the children.

They all sing contemporary praise songs during the service. Some of them are in Tagalog, but the music is the same.

A basket is placed at the front of the church for offering. You go to the front of the church to drop in your gift.

There's an unusual custom in the Philippines of children taking the hand of an older adult and raising it to their (the children's) head for a blessing of some sort. This happens everywhere, not just in church. A few of the children from the church took my hand, put it on their head, and I said something like, "God bless you." It actually felt sort of nice.

In addition to local church worship services, volunteers may experience larger gatherings that are equally fascinating.

Bo Fagin wrote about worship in Senegal:

Woman's Forum. What sort of image does that bring up in your mind? . . . In The United Methodist Church in Senegal, it means a

Saturday spent listening to a sermon, hearing the witness of a lay-woman, playing Bible trivia. These women know more Bible facts than I ever forgot. I had the answer to maybe one in ten, *after* hearing the translation to English from French.

But the African twist to the day was music. We started with singing. That does not mean one hymn. It means twenty to thirty minutes of spirited singing in three or four languages while standing, clapping, dancing. There was a big lunch, rice of course, followed by a session where a three-year-old boy went to sleep on my lap. Okay, I took a short nap too.

But the high point of the day was the closing music. It was the band from another church. Full drum set, keyboard, trumpet, and tambourines. They were *good*. They played on the flat roof of the church, which is actually only a two-story house with a canopy set up on the roof. There was another party going on across the street on their roof. They gave up on their DJ and danced to our music. People were hanging out of windows giving us the thumbs-up sign and clapping along with the music.

At some point a line dance started with people waving handkerchiefs. For those who had none, people were giving out tissues. It was great and went on forever. Well, almost until dark, when I made for home to avoid being lost in the maze of streets that surround the house.

Janine Roberts wrote from Zimbabwe:

At 4:00 a.m. I hear the first rustlings from women sleeping on the floor all around me. After a long drive to the south of the country yesterday, I arrived with some church members at the United Methodist conference. Now, one by one the women begin quietly singing, "*Mangwanani Baba*" (Good morning, Father).... The singing goes on for a while until I open one eye halfway and realize everyone is sitting up in their beds waiting. I begrudgingly pull myself upright. They immediately stop singing and start to pray. They had been waiting for their sister from the United States to wake before beginning morning prayers.

Holidays and Celebrations

A few holidays—primarily Christmas and Easter—are celebrated almost universally where there are Christian communities. However, in countries south of the equator, Christmas is in the summer and Easter in the fall. Mother's Day may be celebrated in September, not in May; and the date for Thanksgiving (or a similar harvest festival) depends on which month marks the end of the harvest season.

Labor Day, a secular holiday, is May 1 in some countries rather than the first Monday of September. Many holidays in the United States are ordinary days elsewhere. (Try asking someone in England, "How do you celebrate the Fourth of July here?")

Nevertheless, holiday celebrations can be a time of fascinating intercultural experiences, and volunteers often find their lives enriched as they interact with people around them in a new way.

For instance, **Mary Osif** wrote of holidays in Poland:

> Some interesting tidbits for you about Polish traditions.... Christmas is spent at some family member's in a village. Food: fish, *pierogies* (filled dumplings), pasta with poppy-seed sauce, and cakes. Twelve dishes are made, and there is always an extra place set for an unexpected guest. All Saints' Day, November 1, is spent going to cemeteries and lighting candles on the graves of ancestors. And lots of prayer. My favorite is Easter Monday. In the Czech Republic on Easter Monday, boys whip girls' legs with sticks. In Poland, everyone just pours water on each other. A cupful, a bucketful, whatever! I am sad I'm going to miss that. I promised the group that I would try to start that tradition in the States. Who's with me?

Holy Week

Bob May wrote from the Philippines:

> Recently at 3:30 a.m. I awoke to the screaming of some unknown woman.... I jumped out of bed and grabbed my clothes. I ran outside to see what was going on. It turns out that Holy Week had started, and the Catholics in this town have a tradition of a continuous "wailing passion" service for the next seven days. It's a live performance from a site unknown to me, but they sang the same "wailing as if you are dying" songs all day and night. They had erected a large loudspeaker

near my room, and it blasted all day. It was not supposed to stop for seven days—twenty-four hours a day! Fortunately (for me) something broke and it stopped after only two days.

All Saints' Day

Julie Meyer explained how All Saints' Day is celebrated in Bolivia:

On November 2, the Day of *Todos los Santos* (All Saints' Day), Doña Agida invited me to spend the day with her family. Since I didn't have class that day, I left early and arrived in time for breakfast. After breakfast, I helped the women prepare the lunch. I washed potatoes in the river, and learned to peel *yuca* (a starchy root).

Meanwhile, many of the men from the *nucleo* (neighborhood) had begun to drink *chicha* (an alcoholic drink). Since I was busy cooking with the women, I was spared having to deal with that problem. It was fun, and I got to know the women of the community a little more. Now I'm able to tell who is married to whom, how many kids they have and their names.

After lunch, we went to the cemetery. The families cover the graves of their loved ones with sweet bread, candy, and in some cases coca leaves and cigarettes. The people of the community make their rounds to pray at each grave and then a family member gives them a plate full of the sweets. At the end of the day, the graves are once again empty. It reminded me a little bit of Halloween and kids going door-to-door for their sweets. The women had their traditional dress of skirts, blouses, and bowler hats, but instead of multiple colors it was all black. Doña Agida took good care of me, telling me what to do and where to go when I was unsure of what to do. Overall, it was an interesting day.

Thanksgiving

Cally Curtis wrote from Belize:

October is the time of celebrating the harvest here. I've never seen services more moving or humbling. At every church, one "Lord's Day" (or Sunday) is set aside for giving thanks for the harvest. The first of the three services is for the boys, the second for the girls, and the last for the youth, choir, men's and women's groups, and other organizations within the church.

The sanctuaries are elaborately decorated. Gigantic bunches of bananas hang over doorways. Every railing and windowsill is lined with hundreds of green oranges. Tied to the end of each pew is an effusive arrangement of magnificent palm fronds and green-and-orange-striped leaves. Above, along a fishing line that stretches over the sanctuary, leafy branches bearing fruit hang in silhouette against the light streaming in from the open windows.

In each service the children, dressed in pressed, clean school uniforms, form a processional to the altar. Two by two, measuring their steps in time to the music, their faces serious and concentrated on this task, they slowly process down the aisle. Infants I are first, then Infants II, all the way up to Form Six. In their arms they carefully balance homemade shoebox baskets decorated with white, pink, and green crepe paper and spilling over with brilliant hibiscus flowers, fruit, vegetables, and green leafy stems.

At the altar, the children form a line facing the congregation. They recite a verse of thanksgiving and sing a chorus of praise, then turn in unison and place their lovely baskets on the altar. As they proceed out, the next group processes in....

How can I express the beauty of basking in the sound and golden light and spectacle of these Harvest Thanksgiving services? My heart is full and grateful to be here.

Becky Harrell described Thanksgiving in Chile:

For the majority of you, it is the second day of feasting. For me ... the day after the feast. Thirty-six ... that's right, thirty-six Chileans adorned my table by sharing with me in giving thanks for all that we have and for one another. To come to a place of feasting requires preparation, and the preparation for Thanksgiving in Chile began the week before.

The guest list came first, but was quickly tossed as invitations were extended to friends met on the street or in the office or schoolyard. It appeared as if fifty or more would actually accept. How do you feed that many people ... and where do you put them? *No importa* (it doesn't matter), as they say here in Chile ... prepare ... that is most important.

And, in the preparation, do you think there were obstacles? Ha! Of course there were! My "week before the event" hunt for a turkey in the Atacama Desert proved futile. Visits to every *Supermercado* (supermarket) in town resulted in no turkey. *No importa.* There was smoked turkey and smoked ham, which ended up freeing me from "stove duty."

Monday was shopping for foodstuffs.... Tuesday was shopping for foodstuffs the *Supermercado* on Monday didn't have.... Wednesday was shopping for foodstuffs the *Supermercados* on Monday and Tuesday didn't have ... learning to substitute field *camote* (sweet potatoes) for yams, using mozzarella cheese when cheddar cannot be found, knowing *salvia* is sage, knowing who owns regular cake pans when they are not sold anywhere in the city....

Friday night arrived, and some guests were *gringo* (North American) by arriving exactly at 8:00 p.m., others were *chileno* (Chilean) and arrived just before 9:00 p.m., some even later....

One guest arrived with his guitar, many brought Chilean wines and Coca-Cola, another came with copies of Christmas songs (in Spanish, of course) ... so as soon as our appetites were satisfied, we leaned back in our chairs to allow our stomachs "room," and began to sing ... all thirty-six voices in harmony, singing of the birth of our Lord Jesus Christ.

Christmas

Stan and Jennie Lowrey told this story about Christmas in the Bahamas:

We went to a very interesting children's Christmas program last Thursday evening at the Methodist Church in Tarpum Bay. The curtain would open on a small child standing alone, who would say a few lines of a Christmas poem, and the curtain would close. Then the master of ceremonies would brag on the performance *and* ask for cash donations in honor of this child!

This went through about twenty children; some did poems, some sang, some danced, and there was a skit by the older children. At the end, the whole choir (thirty-two children) sang a couple of songs. It was a two-hour program. All you Finance Committee members, this is a great place to get fund-raising ideas! We have learned to carry a lot of one-dollar bills.

Jim Gulley, volunteering in Cambodia, wrote:

As I jot this line, Pastor Tan Yong of Toul Kpos United Methodist Church, Svay Rieng Province, has just collected my offering in the midst of their Christmas Service, at which I will be the preacher. Now we will pray over the offering. Done. Children's choir sings.

Our sanctuary is a nightmare for Methodists, Lutherans, and other folks covetous of quiet naves. A chicken has wandered twice now across the (imagined) dais. I sit with my colleague Paul Sithan and Pastor Sok Sovandy on the left front side of an eighteen-by-fifteen-foot shelter. The single-layer palm thatch overlays bamboo strips attached to a bamboo frame, firmly driven into the dirt floor. Our walls: colorful cloth, gently rippling in the morning breeze. Youth choir sings.

We sit in rented blue plastic chairs along with the "overflow" crowd of sixty-plus. The greatest challenge: competing for the airwaves; not so much with the dozen or so cheerful children playing all around, but with the convoy of passing motorbikes less than twenty meters away, brazenly balancing up to fifteen (count them) thirty-liter jugs of fuel being smuggled from Vietnam, a mere ten kilometers away. That took place while I was preaching! Fortunately, Paul, my diminutive interpreter, receives a boost from the PA system, a popular item with Cambodian Methodist pastors to get the word to the community! Three neighboring pastors and two laywomen join Pastor Tan Yong up front to lead us in a hymn. I'm up next. Sermon from Luke 2:1-22: 'Jesus Came for All, Even Shepherds!' . . . Amen—I didn't think you wanted to hear the whole sermon!

Next? Christmas dinner for all who came to the service, prepared by members in pots and pits nearby. Round tables replace the rows of plastic chairs. Three sittings are required to feed everyone. Then comes our turn to eat. Rice, always rice. But also something special: rice noodles made in a local "factory" operated by a woman in a sister congregation some ten-plus kilometers away. Later we see this newly inaugurated small business financed by funds from the General Board of Global Ministries' Women's Division. "Eat more!" urges Mrs. Tep Lonn, passing me the fish sauce that complements the roasted catfish.

New Year's Eve

Ken Ruse wrote about New Year's Eve in Tonga:

I actually stayed up until after midnight just so I could see what takes place in Tonga at midnight on New Year's Eve. I heard a lot of fireworks, and then I went to bed. About two in the morning I was awakened by a group of Tongans standing outside my *fale* (house) singing New Year's songs. The same thing had happened on Christmas Eve night, but at that time, all the songs were Christmas carols sung in English, which I could of course understand. Tonight, I didn't have a clue what they were singing. So I just rolled over and went back to sleep.

Dee Stevens wrote from Honduras:

One of my more inwardly satisfying experiences was New Year's Eve. We all went to a relative's house around 9:00 p.m. All of us (about fifteen) visited and set off firecrackers until midnight. At midnight, we sat down to a wonderful meal of turkey and other delicious foods. Before we started our meal, Reverend Rodas led us in prayer as we thanked God for the gift of family and of a New Year. What a wonderful way to bring in the New Year!

Ramadan

Bo Fagin, volunteering in Senegal, wrote:

The Holy Month of Ramadan is in full swing. The faithful do not eat or drink during daylight hours, but rise early to eat breakfast before sunrise and then eat at least two meals after the sun goes down. It is fun to be out just before it gets dark and to see people buying bread and other food items for the meal that breaks the fast. After sundown it seems like party time, with lots of people on the streets.

Weddings

Bo Fagin also commented on weddings in Senegal:

On Saturday I went to a wedding with Sylvia, my daughter [a Peace Corps volunteer].... We arrived at the location of the reception two hours after the appointed time and found the party still going strong; in fact, dinner was still being served. There was meat *and* veggies in the bowl along with the rice.

Now you ask about the ceremony. Well, so did I. Apparently the men go to the mosque and do the paperwork and then return for the party. I say "apparently," since the groom never did show up while we were there. In former times the bride sat in a room receiving visitors for weeks before the big day. Today it is two days in the village and either two hours or not at all in Dakar. The absence of the groom seemed to pose no problem to the bride, who was walking around talking to people.

By walking around, I mean walking around the neighborhood. There was a tent set up on the street in front of the apartment with a disc jockey and *loud* Senegalese music (always a complicated drum beat). The women danced and got somewhat wild with kicking and rotating of bellies that they bared during the dance. The guys sat on the sidelines and drank tea. I was given a good seat on the sidewalk while Sylvia mingled with the crowd. After a while the *Toobab*'s (foreigner's) presence became normal and I was ignored, except by the people who passed in the street.

Ever forget to buy a wedding gift? No problem in Senegal. I saw a family member buy a bowl and a cover for the bowl from a passing street vendor and present it to the bride. I thought it was pretty funny, but everybody else thought it was normal.

We left after two hours. The disc jockey had packed up his speakers and left, but the party was in full swing and would go on all night. Or so I was told. At one point three women *Greols* (professional singers/storytellers) sang to the bride in Pular. They had *good* voices. It was a quiet, well-mannered party since there was no alcohol and apparently no family arguments to settle.

Patriotic Celebrations

Stephanie Saunders wrote from Chile:

The eighteenth of September, Chile's independence day, is a day which all Chileans await and celebrate as if it were their own birthday or Christmas. Nationalism is strong here. In fact, the government regulations state that all businesses and homes must fly a Chilean flag on the eighteenth. The month is filled with *empanadas* (a type of meat or cheese turnover), *chicha* (a type of sweet wine), and the *cueca* (Chile's national dance).

Becky Harrell, also volunteering in Chile, wrote:

The *21 de Mayo* (May 21) is an important date in Chile's naval history, and it is celebrated with a parade. Each year, a couple of days before the twenty-first, every city in Chile clears her main streets, and all schools within her borders participate. Students are dressed in their freshly pressed uniforms, and teachers don sunglasses, the women slide their purse strap high onto the shoulder and tuck the bag under their arm, and the men coordinate their ties to match the ladies' uniform colors. Bands rally in front of each school group, drumming to a military beat so that marchers know the timing needed to "fall in."

It is very organized, very important, very impressive. Members under the officials' tent have titles and responsibilities that cover regions, cities, government, and public service. As each school passes in review, officials stand to honor the flags they carry and the scholastic excellence they represent.

For the second year in a row, *Instituto Agrícola Kusayapu* (Kusayapu Agricultural School) garnered position number two, and her teachers, students, and missionaries served her proud. The flag of Chile, the *"Wip'ala,"* and the *bandera* (flag) of Kusayapu marched to the beat of the Kusayapu *Laka* (drum) band.... The flags and band were followed by Director José Salgado and his staff of *directivos* (administrators) and teachers, who were trailed, in unison step, by individual volunteers Ann Burger and Ed Benner. Kusayapu students then followed in perfect harmony to the beat of the *Laka* (drum), displaying traditional Andean costumes and dance....

Cameramen scurried to get a shot of this unusual and different group. Normally, the schools pass in front of the officials' tent, then scatter among the hordes of parents and friends for photo ops. But not Kusayapu... she marched along the full length of the *Baquedano* (a main street in Iquique), past university and Ministry of Education offices, past restaurants and ice-cream stands, past street vendors who were waiting for tourists but always maintaining her "beat," she marched all the way to Iquique's town square... to the clock tower. Her students never tired, never stopped; the drummers' arms must have been hurting, the dancers' feet must have been swelling, and the *sampoña* (a wind instrument) players must have been out of wind, but on they marched....

Once we arrived at the *plaza* (main square), Kusayapu stopped in front of the *teatro* (theater), giving others nearby the opportunity to see her fully. Suddenly, a man I presumed to be Chilean extended his hand to me and asked, in English, where I was from.... His accent was certainly *not* Chilean... but Mexican. When I said Texas, his eyes lit up.... "Me too," he said. "Where in Texas?"

I explained I had lived the past twenty-plus years near Ingleside and Corpus Christi. He knew the area well. He was from McAllen. "*No!*" I said. Then I spotted the Rotary International logo. It was *them*... the GSE group from my home Rotary District in Texas. Ha!

I had heard they were coming and would be in Iquique for three days, but with the busyness of work, I had forgotten. And there they were... it was their leader, Joe Aleman, who heard my "Spanglish" and came over to investigate. He was incredibly impressed with Kusayapu and was curious about me and why I was in Chile....

The wonders of a day never cease to amaze me. I am learning it is better not to make too specific your plans for the day. Allowing God room to delight and surprise you has to be the greatest of joys. It has been a good day.

American Holidays

Janine Roberts described spending July 4 in Zimbabwe:

I woke up on the Fourth of July, not even realizing that it was a special day back home. When Nicole [another individual volunteer] and I remembered, we went around wishing everyone a Happy Fourth. Most people thought we were nuts, but maybe they were not so far off the mark!

I did not have too much time to feel sad that I was missing all the festivities at home, though. We stopped by a small supermarket for bread, and playing over the intercom was John Denver's "Country Roads." While walking down one of the aisles, I spotted familiar red, white, and blue. Upon closer inspection, I discovered that it was a bag of cookies called "Kentucky Cookies" with the American flag painted plain as day across the front. Not what I expected to find in a Zimbabwean market. I bought them immediately, and my roommates were entertained for the rest of the day as I sang all the patriotic songs I could remember to the bag of cookies, ending with the Pledge of Allegiance. My anthropology professor will be disappointed that I reverted back to my American ways, but it was only for the day.

Our friend Americo, who is from Angola, decided he would make us a special meal that evening that his mother always made for him while he was growing up in Angola. When he brought it out, we could not believe our eyes. Americo had made an entire pan of potato salad! You can't get much more American on the Fourth of July than potato salad. So, God was watching out for me on what could have been a very homesick day.

Other Cultural Differences

Volunteers are often blessed to be a part of authentic cultural experiences that are possible only for those who live and work among the people. We have enjoyed reading their accounts of cultural differences they have experienced, including the ones below.

Hal and Margaret Waters of Dulac, Louisiana, wrote:

We have experienced a Houma welcome and recommend it. A Celebration for the Elderly, in which we participated, was held right after our arrival in November. The Bayou Eagle Native American Dancers were the highlight of the afternoon. Following a delicious gumbo dinner, the Eagles danced. When the beat of the drum and chant began the atmosphere of the room changed. The head Eagle dancer entered, followed by the Elder Leaders of the Nation and the talented dance troop. We could see and feel the dancers and the audience respond to the dignity and seriousness of the moment. The room was transformed.

Later we were invited to dance. We very much felt that we were for the day a part of the Houma people and culture.

Dominique Gettliffe, of the Democratic Republic of the Congo, wrote:

It's difficult to explain my first impressions in a few words. It's an experience different from any other. I think that in a certain way I am in a state of shock. There are so many images constantly bombarding me:

bicycles loaded with huge bags of charcoal;
huge holes in the roads;
women with their brightly colored dresses;
the Congolese *franc* bills, which are incredibly dirty, smell bad, are sticky, and of which you need handfuls to buy a meal;
the groups of children carrying one another around;
minivans stuffed with twenty people;
Belgian, French, or other neo-colonialists who have lived here for thirty years, and are used to all that;
the dilapidated buildings;
guards opening the gateways of homes and institutions surrounded by high walls;
La Brioche, a café-bakery run by a Frenchman where I have been seeking refuge from time to time;
the old and young men, women, and children who fill the streets and sidewalks, who call and cry out to one another;
the surprise of seeing so many extremely well dressed people, in coat and tie, or dresses with flamboyant designs;
the incredible beauty of certain people;
the emphatic way that the people talk;
seeing [President] Bush in the middle of all that on CNN;
sleeping under a mosquito net, and feeling sweaty all day long;
the fear of taking pictures, and of questioning everything I put in my mouth;
the fact that the average income is less than a dollar a day, in a country that is super-rich in minerals;
working on a covered market project in the midst of all that....

111

Advice for Future Volunteers

Some volunteers have offered advice for future volunteers, which we have shared during orientation/training weekends. Hearing from those who have "been there" makes an impression on those who are preparing to go. Here are some words of wisdom from past volunteers.

Dee Stevens made a list of things she wanted future volunteers to know before heading for Honduras:

> Lessons I Have Learned:
> 1. Motorized vehicles always have the right of way. Pedestrians must move out of the way if they want to see another sunset.
> 2. Never wait to take a shower, etc., if there is water available. At different times of the day, parts of Copán are without water. You never know when it will occur.
> 3. Always have a flashlight in an easily accessible place.
> 4. Never assume purified water will be available.
> 5. Bug soup is not so bad.
> 6. Get used to people being amused with your lack of knowledge about the language and culture.
> 7. Always expect beans, eggs, and corn tortillas and never tire of them or you are in for a long (very long) stay.

Reverend **Marvin Willard**, a retired pastor nicknamed "Marvelous Marvin" by appreciative parishioners during his two years in Belize, wrote about taking too many things with him: "I am painfully aware that I just plain brought too much stuff with me. Dress clothing, like suits and ties, is not appropriate in the tropics."

On the other hand, **Steve Paylor** wrote about things he wished he had brought with him to Chile:

> *More credit cards.* I brought a few, but probably should have brought a second MasterCard/Visa. Had I brought my Citibank MasterCard, I might have enjoyed the luxury of the VIP lounge in the Santiago airport. My Delta SkyMiles-Amex card got me into the

VIP lounge in the international section where I enjoyed free drinks, food, TV, and magazines. Makes that layover all the more bearable. Also, I'm not really sure which of my credit cards allow cash advances because I never use them thusly in the States, which is my segue into:

Bank cards. I brought my ATM card, but just one. What if I lose it? What if it's taken by a malicious machine? Or what happens when they try to send me a replacement in a month or two? (Due to a merger, the bank named on my card doesn't exist except in local memory.)

Long underwear. I have a nice set of this stuff from hiking that's polypro. That's a new word for polyester, though it's woven now. It's great for hiking or outdoors activities because it works when wet. It also dries fast. I've found it super-warm, whether sloshing through a creek underground in a cave or hiking in a snowstorm.

Textbooks. I shrank from buying one before I left because the language is said to be so different between Latin America and Spain, and between Chile and Latin America. But the basics are the same, at least in their rules if not their slang, and I would have had a nice head start in learning if I had started early.

More luggage but not more clothes. I thought it would be better to pack light and get what I needed later instead of filling a duffel bag with all of my clothes. I made two mistakes there. I didn't bring a lot of clothes, and I didn't bring that big duffel bag. It turns out that in the field you can wear your clothes for a week without washing. No one seems to mind, and they don't even appear to smell bad. I never learned that in college and thought I was grungy back home if I wore my khakis twice before washing. I now think all you need is that one warm sweater. But I think you need to have extra space in your luggage so you can take back anything you buy or that is sent to you. I am not sure how I'm going to compress everything, because my bags were full when I got here.

Photos. Photos of family are always appreciated by the people you will be with. And if you play a sport they don't recognize (for me, it's lacrosse), it's helpful to be able to explain what it is.

Books. I think in my haste I assumed I would be so immersed in Spanish that I would trudge through books in Spanish. Ha! Grab some paperbacks and magazines.

Pens and paper. Not that they aren't cheap enough here, but I had so many back home it's hard to buy more.... A pen left out on a table

113

is as tempting here at the school as an open beer at a frat party (disappears quickly).

A volunteer in Bosnia, in an e-mail sent to prospective volunteers, offered the most succinct advice, and possibly the most helpful: "be flexible, have plenty of patience, and go with the flow."

4
Problems and Difficulties

Old-time explorers and colonialists have dubbed Africa all sorts of names, from the "Dark Continent" to the "Lost Continent," and even gone as far as "Hopeless" or "Backwards." Well, this European-American has found Africa to be just the opposite—full of light, hope, and in many ways the only "forward" land in an otherwise upside-down world. In my time here, I have also come to know Africa by my own names and I now call her the "Laughing Continent," as she mocks any semblance of control or ideas I had about order before coming here.
— NICOLE WINDHURST, INDIVIDUAL VOLUNTEER, ZIMBABWE

The life of an individual volunteer is immensely rewarding, always interesting, but not without difficulties and problems. Volunteers have generally reacted with grace and humor to whatever difficulties they encounter. They have also learned to become more dependent on God's grace than on their own resources.

Some prospective volunteers want to go to a particular place and do a specific job rather than trying to find out where they are truly needed. They may expect to do something significant and be appreciated, but find that volunteers are sometimes seen as more of a problem than a help. They may feel that someone is trying to take advantage of them for financial gain.

There may be a need for more complete and accurate information about the work volunteers are to do and their living conditions, and sometimes no orientation is provided upon arriving at the volunteer site.

Volunteers are usually viewed as missionaries, and occasionally an individual volunteer wants to be known as a volunteer and does not wish to be called a missionary, something the host community may find difficult to accept.

Nevertheless, most volunteers are well received. They find fulfilling work, which is appreciated by their hosts, and they develop deep and lasting relationships. Still, the volunteer experience is not without its difficulties. The following examples are indicative of the broad spectrum of challenges faced by individual volunteers.

Water and Electricity

In some places, flipping a switch to turn on the lights or opening a tap to get running water is a luxury only the wealthy can afford. In many places, running water and electricity are available but do not always function as well as they should.

Constance Waddell wrote from El Tabo Methodist Camp in Chile:

Water, water, everywhere . . . but far below us in that incredibly large ocean, there is not a drop to drink—or to use for a shower—or to wash dishes in the sink! The tanks in this Christian camp that Don and I are restoring are totally empty one more time. With thirty-three persons attending a retreat, it is hard not to feel impatient with the answer of Señor Cabes, the man who sells water. "It's not possible until late tonight," he said when Don called. "My water truck broke down and I have to ride a bus to Santiago (two hours away) to get the part." Meanwhile, no one can cook, or flush, or drink that elemental substance—water!

We must be patient. It will be easier for our Chilean guests than for us North Americans. If there is one fruit of the spirit I need daily to receive, it is patience.

So, the other great lesson I'm learning is that patience comes from understanding.

Communications

As a result of insufficient infrastructures, communications can become a major problem, as the following volunteers discovered.

The Reverend **Joyce Mauler Michael** wrote in an e-mail sent from the seminary where she was volunteering in the Czech Republic:

> I was nearly finished with my "Report upon Arrival" when the computer locked up and I lost everything. This happens occasionally with the very old computers that we have here. I will begin the project again, but I may not have time to complete it today. If I cannot finish this report now, I will attempt to send it on Thursday or Friday, if I am able to gain access to the computer room. At any rate, I am trying to get it to you!

We eventually received Joyce's report—by airmail, two months later.

Scott Martin, a volunteer with Food for the Hungry in Nicaragua, wrote: "Our phone is still out of service. It does 'work,' but a recording comes on asking you to dial faster followed by a loud continuous beep, making actual communication very difficult."

Several months later, we heard from Scott again: "After exactly one month, our phone is now restored.... With rare exceptions we have been without a phone for four months."

Dr. **John Clarke**, a volunteer at Maua Methodist Hospital in Kenya, approached communication problems with creativity and humor:

Sending e-mails is often an adventure. The landlines between Maua and Nairobi interrupt your transmission, sometimes as often as every two or three minutes, and at other times I can stay online for an hour or two. . . . One has to develop a real sense of humor about it.

This is entirely typical of almost everything in Kenya. For instance, I am writing this in my flat on Saturday afternoon, and the electricity has been off approximately half of this day, and twice in the last hour. Fortunately my laptop, on which I do my e-mails, has fairly good battery life, and I just keep working with electricity off until I'm out of power.

Travel

Our favorite travel story is the one Yasmine Rana told us about her trip to Bosnia:

When I took my ticket to the airline counter, the agent asked if I was traveling alone. When I said yes, he asked, "Do you have relatives there you will stay with?"

"No, I'm going to work as a volunteer with the United Methodist Committee on Relief," I answered.

He said, "I don't think you should do that, young lady. I want you to go over there and sit down and think about this before you go. It is very dangerous for you to be there alone."

After praying to God to give me direction, I decided to call some people to ask for their advice. If any of them said it was not a good idea for me to go, I would cancel my trip. I called about twenty people, and none of them were at home. Finally, I went back to the ticket counter and told the man I was going. He said, "Well, all right, then. But I'm going to put you in first class."

In Switzerland, where I had to change planes, I went to the ladies' restroom and saw one of my former English as a Second Language students. She and her mother and sister were on their way to Bosnia to visit relatives there. They took me into their family group for the rest of the trip, so I didn't have to travel alone after all.

Travel can be a major challenge, and travel adventures have been the topic of many messages from volunteers.

Miriam Miller, a retiree from Nebraska, drove to her volunteer assignment in Kentucky. She wrote: "I am at Red Bird Mission and all is going well. It was a long two-day trip of 972 miles and I was very tired. But with rest and time all is well. I'm enjoying being back seeing friends and making new friends. There is always work to do. I am well and blessed."

In 2008, Miriam wrote:

> I have just returned from my eighteenth trip to Red Bird Mission since 1996. Being in mission in the Red Bird Missionary Conference is a real joy. The Lord continues to call me to return.... I am willing to do whatever needs to be done, wherever, and there is much variety. I just returned from helping with the Red Bird Missionary Annual Conference meeting at Mary Helen United Methodist Church.... Being at this conference with Bishop King and the sixteen pastors/wives, guests, delegates, the music, and the power of the Holy Spirit in that place was a "Hallelujah" moment.
>
> Since 2001 I have been involved as an Individual Volunteer in Mission at Midwest Mission Distribution Center, Chatham, Illinois. Also, I am a Co-Leader for taking teams of United Methodist Women from Nebraska Conference yearly.... As long as the Lord gives me strength and health I will serve Him where He calls me.

Don White holds the record for distance driven to a volunteer assignment, as far as we can determine. He wrote after arriving in El Salvador from his home in New Mexico: "This notice is to inform you of my arrival in Ahauchapán Friday, November 24, after nine days of traveling in my vehicle for three thousand miles. I am tired but in the hands of El Salvador Christians."

For **Staci Martin,** owning a car in South Africa was a challenge:

> In South Africa, like anywhere else, cars are a status symbol. It seems like everywhere I turn, there is someone washing a car in a parking lot, on the side of the street, just about anywhere. The people who want your business have no shame in telling you directly that your car is a "mess" and "needs a wash."

Diepsloot is dusty and dirty. I don't regularly wash my car because it is pointless. So, on a chronic basis I am told that my car is a mess and needs a wash. I always want to add that it is a "crummy" car, too. But I hold back.

I have washed my car five times in the seven months I have had Midnight Blue (MB). Now, MB never complains, but I know deep down he is ashamed that he is the only one dirty on the road. Sigh.

Last week I had a flat tire and although being an "independent, woodsy, self-contained, no-nonsense woman," I was unable to loosen the tire's bolts. I tried for fifteen minutes and then of course a man arrived and took the bolts off. I figured that I loosened them for him. Under his breath he remarked, "Your car needs a wash."

Julie Meyer traveled to her assignment in Río Colorado, Bolivia, by bus after flying into La Paz. She wrote:

I survived the bus ride from La Paz, and I am going to avoid it as much as possible in the future! I have never seen anything quite like the road before. One lane, and then it drops straight down for miles. When another bus comes, the one going downhill backs up until it finds a space wide enough to let the other one through. I was such a nervous wreck that I didn't sleep the entire trip.

Later, **Julie** wrote about an especially long trip due to the weather:

In my last e-mail, I was still in Trinidad waiting for a bus to San Borja. How bad could it be? Well, I learned the Bolivians aren't joking around when they say that the roads are impassable. I found the only pickup truck making the trip, and a couple of hours into the journey realized what I had gotten myself into. A ten-hour trip ended up lasting three days. I have never seen so much mud in my life! We stripped off our boots (there was really no point), and waded around in mud up to my thighs. There were more than ten people making the trip, so the weight didn't help. . . . It wasn't all bad, though. We spent a great night in San Ignacio de Moros, a beautiful little town. . . . Also, the driver was extremely optimistic and kept everyone's spirits up.

Another problem with riding the bus is the possibility of strikes, as **Judith Richerzhagen** learned in Kenya: "There was a national *mattatu* (bus) strike impacting bus service on Thursday, which looked like it might mean I would have to stay in Maua. Fortunately, the strike only lasted one day. It was a bit unsettling to see pictures of folks pulled out of buses."

Travel difficulties may be compounded by weather conditions. **Frank and Mary Hedgcock** wrote from Bolivia:

> Cobija (where we spent last week) is a buzzing community—both literally (motorcycles) and figuratively (the capital of the Pando District and full of people who are eager to improve their community). Surrounded on three sides by the Acre River and Brazil, it is incredibly isolated. Planes fly in from (and out to) La Paz only on Tuesdays and Fridays. Our Friday flight was rescheduled for early Saturday morning. The following Tuesday flight was canceled. The bus station indicates all trips are canceled until further notice (rainy season makes dirt roads impassable). Even when buses run, it is a steady fifty-eight to sixty-hour trip from Cobija to La Paz.

Solving the mysteries of local transportation systems can be a challenge, as **Jeanie Pennington** discovered in the Czech Republic: "I was worried about getting home. One can ride all three kinds of transportation with one ticket, but it lasts one hour only. Our time had expired on the ticket, and I had no money to buy another one! No problem; we were only three blocks from home, and I did not even know it!"

Sharon Romich wrote from Nepal about using a local mode of transportation:

> There is a whole system of little three-wheeled vehicles that run along with the buses, the *tuk tuks*. They are supposed to hold twelve people in a space smaller than a minivan, almost half that size. Well, what to do when a big foreigner gets in one! I had to learn to duck. The first time I took one I bumped my head hard on the roof going in and out.

One day I wanted to take one to language class. Well, I got on, found a seat, and sat down beside a Nepali man. I was the only woman in the *tuk tuk*. Of course, my legs are a good two inches longer and four inches rounder than the Nepali men's legs are.

There is always a young boy who rides the back step, collecting money and signaling to the driver with a fist bang on the side when it is time to go or stop. He started yelling "*didi*" (older sister) to me and motioning for me to move over. He put another man in a space that was five inches wide. I was tempted to ask the guy if he wanted to sit on my lap, but since it is not acceptable to look a man in the eye, let alone talk to them, I thought I better not.

Soon it was my stop, and I banged on the roof to signal the driver I wanted out. Then I crawled over ten sets of knees through a nonexistent space. What an adventure!

Sharon's story reminded us of what a Jamaican friend said to Jeanie Blankenbaker, who was visiting Jamaica representing the General Board of Global Ministries in her role as Associate General Secretary for Mission Volunteers. As they tried to get into an already full car, Jeanie's friend said to the occupants, "Small yourselves up!"

In Cambodia, local transportation often consists of motorbikes, as **Jim Gulley** pointed out:

Picture it: Jim and Nancy [Jim's wife] scooting around Phnom Penh on a motorbike. Now complete the picture with the rest of normal traffic: a gazillion other motorbikes and "vehicles" of all sorts on the street moving in what at first appears to be random patterns.

It's been surprisingly easy to adjust to motorbikes, cars, and trucks driving slowly toward me, in my lane of traffic, waiting for the opportune time to angle through to their proper lane. Works pretty well, in fact. Other maniac motorcyclists, however, bobbing and weaving around and through traffic at high speed in the same direction, are truly scary! Even more heart-stopping are those playing chicken—literally!—racing straight across intersections without even turning their heads (great peripheral vision an asset!). Thrills—and recently, spills—enough for everyone!

Bob May found it frustrating that drivers of tricycles used for public transportation in the Philippines tried to overcharge him because he was a foreigner:

> It sort of irritates me that tricycle drivers sometimes try to charge me three times as much as any other rider. I always get out and find another tricycle. If that one charges me too much, I get out and find another one. It just aggravates me, but if I let them charge me that, then they'll try the same thing with the next non-Filipino. I guess it's just the principle of the thing. They think I have more pesos than the Filipino riders do, but I'm probably on as tight a budget as they are. Some try to charge me more after the ride. I never pay it then. Even if they start yelling at me like the guy did this evening. Single riders are usually supposed to pay double—Filipino too—but not triple.

One means of travel that is more common in other countries than in the United States is walking. **Sarah Smith** wrote from Peru:

> On Tuesday, Eusebio and I went to the *campo* (country) to visit some of the churches there. There are no Methodist churches within the city of Juliaca—all of them are in little towns in the *campo*. There are two circuits of churches. One is ninety minutes from Juliaca, and the other is eight hours away by bus.
>
> As this was only a day trip, we visited the closer circuit, which has five churches. Since it was a weekday, most people were harvesting potatoes in their fields. After the crowded bus ride from Juliaca, we walked to the churches by way of fields and pastures, and saw many cows, sheep, and pigs....
>
> On our way back toward the highway at the end of the day, we were invited to stop at one family's house to eat potatoes that had been cooked in the ground. It was a long, dusty day, and I was exhausted after walking throughout the day.

The most arduous walk—or rather, climb—was probably that of Reverend **Leta Gorham** in Nepal:

> This month I climbed for five hours, twenty minutes straight up a mountain to a mission hospital. We had driven for five hours to the base

of the mountain in a jeep. My expatriate friends were taking bets that I'd have to be carried part of the way or take ten hours as did the last woman of only forty-eight years of age. [Leta was sixty-five at the time.] In contrast, my Nepali friends sought another way to handle my risk-taking. They actually prayed that I would not fall off the mountain. Even a Hindu friend told me, "I did what I think you Christians call *pray*."

All supplies for the hospital or anything else must be carried the same route up. Sick and injured people in hammocks slung over the shoulders of two to four men and/or women arrive each day. This is the local "ambulance." Some have been carried for days. When traffic seems bad on your local expressway or you must pause to let an ambulance pass, silently say a prayer for the Nepali who is seriously ill or has a broken bone and is being jostled up the mountain to a hospital.

A fifty-eight-year-old woman from England and I returned down the mountain on foot where we met the local bus and rode for two of the five hours back to Kathmandu on top of the bus—no rails—in the winter wind. The first hour we were joined "cozily" by thirty Nepali men on top and sixty-plus people inside the bus.

For volunteers who work in a country other than their own, air travel is usually a necessity. It often brings its own complications, and is sometimes the most grueling part of the volunteer experience.

Air travel after September 11, 2001, has meant dealing with increased vigilance at airports, sometimes causing problems when leaving or entering a country. **Don White,** en route to Palestine, encountered a major problem: "I arrived Wednesday and am okay here. The security in Los Angeles took away my *new* computer. More news later." Several years later, we learned that Don did not see his computer again until he returned to the Los Angeles airport the following year. When he got it back, it had been programmed in Hebrew.

"Will there be someone to meet me at the airport?" is a common cause for concern as volunteers travel to unfamiliar places where they do not yet know anyone. Uusally they find a warm reception, and up to now no one has failed to find the way to their place of service.

Mary Osif described her arrival for service in Poland as pleasant:

> A layperson from the Methodist Church in Ostroda named Adam met me at the airport with one of those little signs that limo drivers have: "Mary Osif—United Methodist Church." He spoke nearly perfect English, as he had lived in the States for a few months and is actually a teacher at the language college here. It was quite a long drive from Warsaw to Ilawa, but we talked a lot and after we picked up his wife, I managed to sleep a little in the car. We got to the parsonage around eight o'clock at night, where Pastor Kris and his wife had some supper waiting for us.

Some plane rides are just plain scary, like the one **Sandy Rowland** experienced on her way home from Puerto Rico: "I made it home safely after some turmoil at the airport and riding through a thunderstorm in the sky. It was beautiful, but when the pilot said, 'Everyone sit down and fasten your seat belts tightly around your waist,' I started to pray."

Another return trip brought a different kind of problem for **Dan and Nona Shelly**, flying home from Kenya:

> Our mission to Kenya was a wonderful and very productive trip. Unfortunately, Dan sat next to three girls returning from Croatia on our way back across the Atlantic. Their whole group had gotten sick during their trip, and they decided to share it with him. So today is the first day that he feels semi-human again.

Dangers and Catastrophes

Sometimes a volunteer candidate (or a candidate's parent) has asked, "Can you guarantee that I (or my son or daughter) will be safe if assigned to that place?" Our answer has to be, "No. We cannot guarantee that anyone will be safe anywhere—not even in your own hometown. What we can guarantee is that God will be with you, no matter what happens, and that we and many others will be praying for your safety and well-being."

Of course, some places are more dangerous than others, and we have tried to make sure that potential volunteers are aware of the possible risks. Remarkably, in spite of having been involved in catastrophic natural disasters and exposed to warlike conditions, individual volunteers have thus far escaped fatal injuries while on their volunteer assignments. We thank God for the protection that has been afforded them.

Part of the orientation/training is a session on "Safety and Security," an effort to provide volunteers with the information they will need to stay as safe as possible while traveling and working in unfamiliar settings.

In a place where missionaries are evacuated because of potential life-threatening circumstances, individual volunteers are evacuated along with the missionaries. In situations where there are no missionaries, if United States citizens are being evacuated, volunteers must make their own arrangements to go to the nearest safe place.

In this section we will discuss several types of dangers that have been faced by individual volunteers.

1. Natural Disasters

In some parts of the world, one of the perils confronting volunteers is the occurrence of earthquakes, as the following excerpts indicate.

From a New Mexico newspaper article about **Don White**, a volunteer in El Salvador:

> The most severe and widespread of the recent earthquakes was the one that got it all started January 13. It was a Saturday and Don White had planned to make the two-hour drive "to the ocean" with a group of the teens he was teaching. White describes the group's destination as a waterfall and canyon area.
>
> White never made the trip, though. While trying to open a barbed-wire gate to reach a church where he was to pick up some of the teens, he bent down and snagged his ear on the sharp points of the fence. He was bleeding profusely enough to force him to return to his local home

to tend to his injured ear. He still had thoughts of making the trip, but his hosts—in a country always leery of diseases like hepatitis—convinced him to forgo his plans.

So White stayed home, spending part of his afternoon chatting with "another Gringo," as White puts it. During their conversation, the other man mentioned the "slight tremor" the area had felt the previous week.

White started to respond, "and before I could get the sentence out, the earth began to shake," he recalls. He thought, "That was good for a demo."

But this was no demonstration. This was very real. All too real.

The earthquake registered 7.6 in magnitude and killed 844 people. Six of the dead were teens who had gone to the waterfalls in the canyon where White had intended to go that day. He later learned that "the mountain fell over." He believes he would have been one of the casualties had he made the outing that day.

The quake, centered on the ocean floor off the country's coast, injured 1,800, damaged or destroyed 280,000 dwellings, and left 1.2 million people homeless. During the quake, White stood in the doorway of his home and watched as people poured into the streets "with eyes wide open," he says. Many had their mouths open, but they weren't talking.

"You see it on TV," White says of news reports, "but it's different. There's not good language to describe it. It's the most unstable feeling in the world. When Mother Earth starts to move underneath you, nothing else has any meaning."

Becky Harrell wrote of her experiences in Chile:

The moving of the earth is an extraordinary thing, and there are scientific reasons for it. Our earth is alive and that movement is evidence of it.

Arriving at Kusayapu Agricultural School and Pachica, the nearby town, only one week after the devastation of a 7.9 earthquake, our current work team from Texas has experienced life in a very different way. They are working to restore life by repairing broken water mains miles away that are the source of potable water. . . . They are removing fallen rock and boulders from a damaged water canal. Water is the source of life in the Tarapaca Canyon. Water is needed in the agricultural fields to provide food and a livelihood for many. Clean, potable water is needed for the health and life of men, women, and children that live in Pachica and work and study at Kusayapu.

2. Accidents

Although accidents involving individual volunteers have been mercifully rare, they do happen—sometimes while serving, but even more often after returning home.

Yasmine Rana suffered a serious accident in her hometown:

I just woke up and have been forcing myself to move around, though everything hurts. One takes for granted all the things one does. Just now I realize how much effort it is to do the simplest things: get into bed, brush my teeth, raise my arm, take a shower, go up and down the stairs.

I can't believe this happened. I was walking on a beautiful Saturday morning, in the crosswalk, on my light, when a car was turning, wouldn't stop, and hit me. I flew onto her hood, into the air, spun around, and then rolled around the road's pavement several times before stopping sprawled in the center.

Since it was an area with some shops and apartments, people came running out. I was screaming and crying from the shock. My arm was bloodied, and I could barely move. A man, from nowhere, ran to me and held my hand the entire time. He was a stranger. Another man came to me and took my cell phone from my pocket to call my family. The police came. One officer held my head and assured me I would be fine, then the ambulance came. . . .

They took me to a local hospital. Since I was hit in the kidney area, I couldn't leave without a urine test, to check for blood. The officer told me he gave the woman a summons, but she said she didn't see me. I don't know how she couldn't see me. I just remember lying on the ground, with the stranger holding my hand, and the officer holding my head, and looking into the blue sky, watching the clouds move, and thinking this was a perfect day, all except for this.

I'm making myself move, despite the pain. My face has no marks or scratches. The bruises are on my back—where I have tire track marks, swelling in my legs, and my right arm lost a lot of skin—which

I know will grow back eventually. She hit me on my left side, so that's pretty sore. I had no broken bones—I have no idea why. I had no internal injuries—I have no idea why. I was literally thrown into the air and smashed onto the ground. It was like a bad dream—too unreal.

Not all volunteers have been as fortunate as Yasmine. One volunteer who traveled frequently to Mexico was killed in an accident at his home in Texas in 2005, when his van fell off the jack and onto him while he was changing a flat tire, crushing his chest and causing his untimely death. Another, who had volunteered in Honduras, was killed in a collision while driving near his home in Missouri. A third died in a traffic accident in Cambodia, where he was working after having served as a volunteer with Heifer Project International in Vietnam.

A heart attack, rather than an accident, caused the death of a volunteer who had served for several months in his native country of Fiji and had returned home to Seattle, Washington, for Christmas, planning to return to Fiji with his wife, who had stayed home to finish the year at her nursing job. The most recent death of a former volunteer, to our knowledge, is the passing of Reverend **Paul Perry** of Austin, Texas, following a long and valiant struggle with cancer.

The most serious accident we have heard about from any of the individual volunteers while on assignment is the following account from **Leta Gorham** in Korea.

I remember writing to you on my sixty-fifth birthday from the top of the world in Nepal—a time engraved forever in my heart. And now I write to you from a country with mountains everywhere just like Nepal but quite a few feet shorter. Recently, however, as I tumbled and hit and jerked against trees being uprooted and rocks and sticks and poles hitting me everywhere, I seemed to be again on the highest mountain in the world. Finally, I felt arms enfold me and stop my fall and gentle words, "Stay calm, Mom, stay calm."

Yes, I had fallen a great distance, and then arms held me with my head an inch or two from an enormous rock that could have been the end of this life. Yes, my spiritual son, Reverend Jeong, had risked his life to save me. When he saw me slip—quite by accident, for he was ahead of me on the trail—and turned to look just as I fell, he literally threw himself after me; as he said, "I flew with you, Mom."

When we looked at the stone, Han said, "It is a miracle, Mom; we have walked in the shadow of death." It truly is a miracle. A team of emergency workers carried me up the mountain and I was treated by the chief, who said, "Hallelujah, your family is waiting below." Yes, how comforting to hear from a stranger. I surely was not alone.

A helicopter flew me to the nearest level space where the ambulance took me to the nearest hospital. My left arm was broken, and my right leg was damaged. I couldn't use it for four days—still can't for more than fifteen to twenty minutes at a time. Something big pierced the bottom of my chin and cut into the bottom of my mouth which was swollen like you can't imagine. I could not open it but a little, and that was to spit out blood in great quantities (which I was told saved much greater damage to my face). It has required considerable surgery. I was totally black from the nose down, and people gasped when they saw me.

I am now in the third hospital, and should be home soon. Most of my students saw their teacher lifted by ropes on national TV, and now all Koreans know where Wesley Mission School is. I should be back teaching soon, and I thank God for a new teacher from Texas who joined us two weeks ago. I thank God always for these wonderful Korean people who shower me always with gifts of love. And then I must fall on my knees (if it were possible) and thank God for a spiritual son whom I didn't even know eighteen months ago who was willing to give his life for me.

3. Crime and Violence

Volunteers sometimes witness violence and occasionally are themselves victims of crimes. We received word from the UMCOR volunteer coordinator for eastern Europe that a volunteer in the Republic of Georgia had been mugged. We telephoned the volunteer immediately, and she told us she had been robbed in a dark hallway leading to her apartment. However, she had followed the instructions given to her at the orientation/training session and left her passport and most of her money in a safe place, so the robber was able to take only the small amount she had with her. Although still shaken by the experience, she was grateful that it was not as bad as it could have been.

Dee Stevens wrote while still in language school at the beginning of her first year of volunteering in Honduras:

> This past weekend was kind of rough. There is a festival going on in Copán. It attracts people from the villages in the mountains. Copán is usually safe because of all the tourists.
>
> Friday night I left the festival around 9:30 p.m.... I did not see (actually, I wasn't even paying attention) three men, strangers from the mountains, following me.... My teacher saw me leave and saw the men trailing me in the dark streets, so he started out after me. Enrique prevented me from being robbed.
>
> On Sunday, two men entered a restaurant and ambushed five men. I am not exactly sure why.... What I know and saw is four men dead in the restaurant and one man mortally wounded. I now know what a person who is shot in the head about an inch above the eye looks like.

Later, while vacationing in Guatemala, Dee again had a frightening experience:

> Antigua is famous for bandits. Our tour bus (school bus) going up the mountain to reach the site of Pacaya was not immune to this unpleasant feature of Guatemala. *Ladrones* (thieves) were in the overhanging trees. As the bus can only go a few miles an hour around the difficult curves of the mountain, huge rocks were hurled at our bus.
>
> As a loud pop sounded and the windows shattered, we (French tourists and I) thought it was gunshots, so we hit the deck. Thankfully, the driver had the sense to keep moving up the mountain. We then saw the rocks on the floor.
>
> A guy sitting across from me was hit with shattered glass on his face. He is okay. I was hit with the shattered glass from his window. It mainly got on my clothes, though a few shards found their way to my left arm.
>
> Luckily, no one was hit in the head by a rock, as it would have killed anyone in its path.

Political violence affects some volunteers. The situation in Zimbabwe has developed into a warlike state that affects even the volunteers who have returned home but continue to work with the people in Zimbabwe. One example comes from **Frank and Wini Dressler**, former Zimbabwe volunteers:

> We just heard from a good friend (who we will try to get to the States next year to earn a PhD) about current conditions there. He said that all those who live on campus are, in effect, under house arrest. Teachers are being harassed . . . and even charged with outrageous acts they never committed. One teacher was badly beaten and elsewhere another teacher was killed. Why? It is assumed that anyone with an education will vote for the opposition party at this month's elections. Can you imagine trying to educate kids under these conditions? Please join your prayers with ours for the safety of the people in our mission schools.

Faced with such a dire situation, one longtime volunteer in Zimbabwe took action that led to his arrest and deportation. An Africa University Contacts Group e-mail about **Gil Gilman**, an individual volunteer in Zimbabwe, reported:

> Harare—An American teacher arrested for filming police demolishing the shacks of urban poor pleaded guilty on Monday to breaking censorship and immigration laws.
>
> Howard Smith Gilman, 68, an unpaid geography lecturer at The United Methodist Church's Africa University, was arrested on May 27 and originally charged with breaking the country's draconian media laws.
>
> His lawyer said he was fined Z$100,000 (US$11) on the immigration charge, Z$200,000 (US$22) on the censorship charge and will be deported from Zimbabwe.
>
> Gilman was held in prison for 10 days after he was arrested filming police destroying the shacks of poor people in Mutare, 400 kilometers east of Harare.
>
> According to United Nations estimates, the blitz by police in what the government calls a cleanup campaign has left 200,000 people

homeless and has led to the arrest of at least 30,000 street traders with no other source of income.

Gilman's lawyer, Innocent Gonese, told the court Gilman was on the board of an orphanage at Mutare and was helping 73 children with their education expenses.

Don White, a volunteer in Palestine, described a country under siege:

> This morning we went a roundabout route to Jerusalem to avoid Israeli checkpoint security. While most staff attended a Baptist church, I visited a Palestinian Nazarene church in the Arab section. This large (for Protestants here) three-hundred-seat building is near the YMCA not far from the old wall. The young pastor and marvelous piano player are also Bethlehem Bible College students and followed stateside service format albeit Arabic music and language.
>
> At service end the piano player (my day's guide) and I were in a parking lot—he was listening to news about an explosion we heard. A suicide bomber again near the site where I was last Sunday—so I'll not linger as long as previously there. An immediate report of forty-two casualties.
>
> Our return home was punctuated with prayer and much circuitousness and even reversals (seeing roadblocks ahead) because three of our van passengers didn't have passage papers. Our two Arab men were today high on the Jewish hate list. Even they were scared! At Bethlehem's final checkpoint our Bethlehem Bible College window sign and two American passports seemed to allow our five Arabs innocence by association. . . .
>
> This is a naturally beautiful place, but the energy spent in dodging bullets spoils the scene.

Nepal has been another perennial trouble spot. **Sharon Romich** referred to the problem of violence there when she wrote:

> There is much Maoist activity in the area. The Maoists are not connected with China but are a homegrown group of guerrilla fighters who are supposedly fighting for more rights for the poor. But they

133

extort money and "recruit" young people at gunpoint. Since Maoist activities have increased around Tansen, the local police chief told the director of the hospital to stone any Maoists who might show up at the hospital. The doctor replied, "We are here to heal, not to kill."

Sharon's second time in Nepal started off with a political crisis. She wrote:

I am staying in Kathmandu with a friend until I go back to Tansen. Last night we heard sirens and helicopters all night, very unusual even though Kathmandu is the capital. We awoke this morning to a news bulletin saying the king, queen, and both royal princes and a grandchild were dead. The story is that the older royal prince was very upset with his parents as they were not giving approval to his relationship with a young woman, and he shot them all and then killed himself. What a tragedy for this little country!...

There are huge throngs of people roaming the streets, mostly young men, it seems. There were huge processions last night to the Bagmati where the royal family was cremated. Now there are curfews every evening, and we are advised by United Mission to Nepal to leave our homes only when absolutely necessary. I am hoping to join a carload of people going to Tansen tomorrow and get out of Kathmandu and off to start my work at the Tansen Nursing School.

4. Critters

On a lighter note, many volunteers have encountered various forms of wildlife. A few of their accounts follow.

Nicole Windhurst wrote from Zimbabwe:

I have a solemn unspoken covenant with the insects and spiders of Zimbabwe—if they stay out of my sacred places (the underwear drawer, cookie jar, under the toilet seat lid, etc.), then I allow them to live *quietly* in the marginalized areas (ceiling corners, under the sofa, behind the fridge, etc.). The unmerciless consequence for even a minor violation is a swift (but dignified) death by aerosol. (Sorry if this offends any of you live-and-let-livers...).

Bob May wrote of his experience with insects in the Philippines:

> It's impossible to escape the little red ants. They are everywhere. They will find any food item within a half hour of my setting it down. They love mango juice. They like toothpaste too. Every morning I have about a dozen ants on my brush. I just cover them with toothpaste and brush on.
>
> Sometimes there will be hundreds of these little red searcher ants running around. The colony must send them out to try and find food for everyone else. I guess they aren't sure where to go, so they look everywhere—like all over my notebooks or textbooks. I might find them in my clothes or crawling through my computer keyboard. I like the way everyone treats the insects and lizards. They just ignore them.

A volunteer in Bolivia wrote: "So, I got up this morning and there was a lizard just hanging out on my toothbrush. Just sitting there on the bristles. And the worst part was, it didn't even faze me. I was just like 'Oh, a little lizard. Isn't that cute!' "

5. Illness

Being sick is never pleasant. Being sick in a strange place can be terrifying. Yet the very circumstance of being in a new place, exposed to new forms of bacteria, almost guarantees that illness will be a part of the volunteer experience. Most of the time the illness is not serious enough to be a major concern, but occasionally a volunteer does have to be hospitalized.

One volunteer in Africa had a severe intestinal infection and was hospitalized:

> I spent from Monday morning until Wednesday morning in the hospital. I had a stomach infection that was quite bad. However, I recovered quickly. (The doctor said I was supposed to be on a liquids-only diet, but I convinced a nurse that I should have fish and mashed potatoes—and it was fine. The doctor walked in and saw my meal half eaten and said, "Well, carry on.")

135

Becky Harrell, who learned while in Chile that she needed breast surgery, made the decision to have the surgery there, and found that she was well cared for both in the hospital and during her recuperation afterward:

> God has kept me at peace in all of this, and I will most assuredly let you know the status as things progress. I am comfortable at the present with remaining here and continuing my work even if treatments are necessary. I have insurance, which should cover the costs. God is with me and I feel his hand and love.

6. Loneliness and Homesickness

An almost universal problem of volunteers, especially those who go as individuals rather than couples or families, is loneliness. Homesickness is also likely to occur, even when the volunteer is enjoying the adventure of being a volunteer and finding real satisfaction in the volunteer work. Quotes from some of the volunteers speak eloquently of the twin problems of loneliness and homesickness.

Florrie Snow wrote while volunteering in El Salvador: "Today I miss my husband, Arturo, terribly. My cellular telephone looks like something from *Star Trek*. Maybe I should open it and say 'Beam me down' and see if it works that way."

Barbara Meijer wrote from Chile: "It's not always easy without my family, my friends and my boyfriend, but I can always talk with God. He carries me."

Stephanie Saunders, another volunteer in Chile, soon after Barbara Meijer left for her home in the Netherlands, told us how much she was missing Barbara, especially because they could speak English together. Even though she spoke fluent Spanish, she found herself seeking out people with whom to speak her own language. Many volunteers have found that when living and working in another country, opportunities to communicate in one's native language are a welcome relief and can be a great blessing.

7. Dealing with Poverty

Bishop Arthur Kulah of Liberia, at one of our orientation/training weekends, reminded us that being a volunteer is a privilege that not many people in the world can afford, since in order to volunteer one must have enough income to travel and to pay one's living expenses while working without pay. Because volunteers are usually much better off than the people they have agreed to serve, it can be an emotional strain to witness the poverty around them.

Volunteers realize how fortunate they are when they see how hard life can be for people who are poor. **Frank and Mary Hedgcock** shared their observations on life in Bolivia:

> We are wealthy beyond belief to most of our neighbors. Some of them sell food or handicrafts on the street. Men shovel sand from the river bottom into their trucks and sit along the highway in front of the school all day waiting to sell it. Whole families of ten or twelve people live in one or two rooms measuring four meters by four meters, sometimes without a bathroom. Some homes have dirt floors and no glass or screens on the windows. The average urban wage is the equivalent of US$70 a month. Unemployment is very high—at least 20 percent—and underemployment is probably 50 percent.

Volunteers from the United States, who are seen as wealthy in many other countries, are often approached with requests and even demands for financial assistance. In places where there are many beggars, it may be difficult to determine who is truly in need. Reverend **Marvin Willard**, a pastor serving in Belize, found it hard to avoid being taken advantage of:

> Beggars on the main streets everywhere. Women with children are especially hard to pass or to say no to. Church members are able to identify the regulars who are on dope (crack mostly). Several panhandlers have come to the door with good stories. In sharing these stories with colleagues, they say that I was taken in.

Bob May found a similar situation during his time in the Philippines:

> I seem to be running into more and more street-children beggars. I
> don't know how to handle them. I am on a missions journey, so I feel
> like I have some sort of responsibility but am not sure what to do. The
> folks here tell me to ignore them. I gave some money to one in Manila,
> and immediately ten surrounded me.

On the other hand, people living in poverty are often extremely
generous toward visitors, as **Burt and Rita Lowe** learned in Kenya:

> For weeks Lydia, our twice-a-week house girl, had been asking us
> and the English missionary couple . . . to come meet her family and
> have Sunday dinner. . . . We bumped down the dirt road and arrived
> about 12:30, parked outside an "entrance," and entered the "com-
> pound." What a greeting we received! A smiling Lydia and her hus-
> band, Julius, and behind them several other family members: Isiah and
> his pretty wife and baby; Cella, Burt's secretary; several other young
> adult relatives; and about twenty-five wide-eyed children who all
> seemed to be between about two and ten. . . .
>
> This compound is much smaller than the spacious yard surround-
> ing the house we occupy. I'm guessing there were eight or ten small
> tin-roofed "houses," a small barn, three cows, hens and baby chicks
> everywhere. . . . Lydia's home was one of the bigger and "fancier" of
> the houses. We sat in her living room. There was a couch, two chairs,
> a coffee table, a buffet, and three stools. That left about two square
> feet of open space.
>
> The four visitors, Lydia, Cella, Lydia's three children, and Cella's
> two all ate in and around the coffee table. The men ate in the kitchen
> but joined us for a birthday cake and some simple toys for Lydia's
> Moses, who was five last week. Everyone was so proud to have us
> there, and we adjourned to the outside and had our pictures taken with,
> it seemed like, *everyone*!
>
> We went home with two large containers of leftover rice and
> mashed potatoes and beans to split between us. . . . One of the family
> chickens had been killed for the occasion—cut into small pieces and
> not a scrap of that was uneaten. . . .
>
> With all those mouths to feed, *we* ended up with the leftovers.

138

8. September 11, 2001

The terrorist attack on the World Trade Center in New York on September 11, 2001, profoundly affected the volunteers who were in other countries as well as those in the United States. One volunteer was on her way home from Nepal and was delayed for several anxious days in Hong Kong. Another had left Korea to renew his visa and return to complete his volunteer service. He wrote from Thailand:

> What I understood from yesterday's visit to the Korean Embassy here in Bangkok is that due to the events in New York on September 11, and based on the increasing number of specific threats that the United States' military bases are receiving in South Korea's capital city, Seoul, let alone the hostilities against Americans that are being asked of Muslims around the world by the Taliban government, the single entry tourist visa applications are being thoroughly reviewed and scrutinized for safety concerns. I interpret that as a decrease in the number of tourist visas given to single travelers with limited funds and no employment in South Korea.... I should know more about my tourist visa Wednesday afternoon.

The visa was never granted, and he was not able to return to Korea to continue his volunteer work.

Nicole Windhurst sensed solidarity from the people of Zimbabwe:

> The response in Zimbabwe was overwhelming—everyone I know is extremely concerned and sends deep condolences. We have held touching memorial services here in the memory of those who lost their lives and have been praying for peace in the United States and the world. I also pray that the intensity of this horrible event would not lead people to anger, revenge, or violence, but instead remind all of us how extremely fragile and precious life is and commit ourselves to preserving innocent lives everywhere in the world.

Howard Pisons and Cheryl Lafferty heard the news while in Chile:

Many chills and much shock here! One teacher told about the devastation at 11:00 a.m., but I didn't quite understand her. From her description, I thought a plane wing had tipped a building in the Twin Cities....

The chaplain rushed up to ask me if I was aware of what happened and I thanked him but figured I would understand more from the CNN in English. I came home and found Howard glued to the TV with tears in his eyes.

He sat there in shock for about five hours. I, on the other hand, couldn't keep watching it. I went to my last three classes. I looked at those little faces and tears welled up as I thought about the families that had been affected by this tragedy.

We watched the TV endlessly and felt *so* homesick. Then I asked our friends if they would like to participate in a small prayer vigil. So I attempted to pray in Spanish.

I prayed for the lost lives, the rescue workers that so relentlessly tried to help, the victims of the hijacking, and the massive destruction that we saw in New York and the collapse of part of the Pentagon. Odd. Difficult to believe it was real.

I prayed for peace in the world. I prayed that we don't develop the same hatred that inspired the attack on America.

A year later, on September 11, 2002, **Becky Harrell** wrote from Iquique, Chile:

September 11 has been an important date here since 1973. It was the day Pinochet overthrew the socialist government of Allende....

This morning, at 8:40 your time, fifteen hundred students and about seventy-five teachers and staff gathered in the outside courtyard of the school. The principal of the school, the head of the English department, and the district superintendent of the Methodist Church [of Chile] asked me to join them and we made our way to the balcony area.

In complete silence, these students stood ... students from pre-K through twelfth grade. The principal began to speak, explaining how blessed this school has been since its inception in 1885 to have volunteers from the United States leave the comforts of their home and country to travel here, to Iquique, Chile, and offer their services, their hearts, and their time. She reminded the students of the tragedy that took place at the Pentagon, in Pennsylvania, and at the World Trade Center last year and of the three thousand persons who died. And of the pain and loss the citizens of the United States have felt.

The district superintendent spoke words of comfort. We all bowed our heads for one minute of silence. The only sound was a mourning dove in the distance. Afterward, many students made their way to me to express simply, with a kiss and a look, their sorrow for our pain. Pain that belongs not only to us, but to the entire world.

Today helped me realize how our neighbors in this world share our loss. Chile is dealing with their memories of September 11 as we will continue to find ways to deal with ours.

5

The Value of Volunteering

Come, you that are blessed by my Father, inherit the kingdom pre-
pared for you from the foundation of the world; for I was hungry and
you gave me food, I was thirsty and you gave me something to drink,
I was a stranger and you welcomed me, I was naked and you gave
me clothing, I was sick and you took care of me, I was in prison and
you visited me.

—MATTHEW 25:34-36

When volunteers describe their volunteer experiences, whether on a weekend mission thirty miles from home or after months or years as individual volunteers in a faraway place, the most frequently used phrase is, "I received so much more than I gave." Volunteers understand the meaning of Jesus' words, "It is more blessed to give than to receive" (Acts 20:35), because they have learned that it is in giving that we receive God's most abundant blessings.

Volunteering is also valuable to persons who receive the volunteers and to those who have a part in sending them out. In the early church,

when Paul and Barnabas returned to Antioch after their first missionary journey, "they called the church together and related all that God
had done with them, and how he had opened a door of faith for the
Gentiles" (Acts 14:27). The Gentiles and the Antioch congregation
received God's blessing through the volunteer service of Paul and
Barnabas.

Bob May, whose path to becoming a career missionary began with
a six-month stay in the Philippines as an individual volunteer, wrote
a summary of what he learned from that experience, which includes
almost all of the values of volunteering that will be discussed in this
chapter:

> I learned that for me missions is a three-part challenge:
> 1. *Serving*—as a mission volunteer teacher, I was not there to pro-
> mote my own skills or accomplishments. I was not there to trumpet
> my degrees and awards. I was there to serve the people in whatever
> way God planned. This meant much more than showing up in a class-
> room several times a week. It was a full-time job, twenty-four hours a
> day, seven days a week. I knew I was representing everybody in Amer-
> ica and everything that being a Christian stood for—the Christian's
> life is the world's Bible.
> 2. *Sharing*—my experience in the Philippines was definitely not a
> one-way exchange of ideas. The Lord used the Filipinos to share so
> much about life and about him. In every experience I feel like I learned
> more than I taught, and I received more than I gave.
> 3. *Loving*—nothing is good that cannot be practiced in love. This is
> the heart of Christianity and missions. No matter what our situation, no
> matter what circumstance we are in, our love of the Lord secures our
> work and us. For me, Galatians 5:13 sums it up best by saying, "Serve
> one another in love."

The Filipinos taught me to be less selfish. I was surprised by how
thoughtful they were. They have a word called *pasalubong*, which
means the gift that you bring back to your family or friends whenever
you go somewhere. This really typifies the Filipino people.
Pasalubong was part of their daily life. Seldom did a Filipino go somewhere that they did not bring a little something back for their friends.

I hope that I take a bit of the selflessness of the people back home with me.

This experience afforded me the time necessary for proper spiritual reflection and meditation. Taking time away from the distractions of my busy American life, I settled into a comfortable Filipino pace. It gave me the opportunity to communicate with the Lord—not only asking through prayer, but also listening to his reply. I found time to listen to God and his direction. My soul and faith were restored and strengthened, but I was challenged almost every day. My journal entries record the struggles that I faced and how my spirit responded.

Through these tests, I became more dependent on the Lord and less dependent on me. This may have been the greatest good of my stay in the Philippines. I learned how special and important a privilege we have in talking to our Creator and being faithful to his will.

There are three groups that are responsible for my mission experience:

1. *The Lord.* The Lord is everything. Without him nothing is possible. I felt his love, his power, and his glory throughout my stay. He provided the call and the opportunity.

2. *The Filipino people.* Without the local support of an American group to ease my transition into the culture, I had to become totally dependent on the assistance and kindness of my hosts. Although this was a little frightening at first, it allowed me to further experience some of God's blessings. I had to grow immeasurably in faith. I had to put my trust totally in the hands of the Lord through the Filipino people. I knew that whatever I accomplished was done only through the Lord and not of my own merits.

3. *My spiritual support family back home.* A surprising benefit of my stay was that I became closer to the people I left behind. When I left for Cabanatuan City, I thought I was leaving my friends and family, but I was wrong. They made sure that we went through all of my adventures together. They were as much a part of the experience as I was. I had never known such an awesome display of kindness. Although I was far from home and distant from them, I never felt alone. I always sensed their wonderful love and support. I felt their care and concern. I read their words of encouragement. I opened their care packages. Most of all I benefited from their prayers. I knew that no matter what happened, I had the prayers of many voices uplifting my service.

Volunteering Benefits the Host Community

The value of volunteering is not limited to what the volunteers gain from the experience. We have often reminded volunteers that their service has also been a great blessing to the people who benefited from their volunteering. The work of the volunteers is beneficial to the host community, sometimes in ways far greater than expected. We have received many heartfelt letters of thanks from supervisors of the volunteers' work. Two examples follow.

After **Sharon Romich** left Nepal, we received this message from the principal of Tansen Nursing School:

> I am writing this just to make an attempt to put into words my heartfelt thanks to you for letting Sharon come to rescue us in the midst of a crisis situation in terms of shortage of teachers and the country's situation itself. Sharon helped us with the first "Nursing Care of Children" course taught at our Tansen Nursing School. She taught in the classroom and guided students in the clinical area in the hospital. Her role was of a teacher, a supervisor, a researcher, an adviser, a facilitator, a leader, and above all a role model to follow.... She has set an example of loving, compassionate, and quality nursing care.

Daniel Martínez, director of La Granja Agricultural School, Nueva Imperial, Chile, wrote about the Christian witness of **Don White**:

> I would especially like to note the excellent contributions of our beloved brother Don White, whom we have come to know little by little, to the point of loving and admiring him very much for his artistic knowledge and even more for his Christian spirit. He is a man of God with a strong faith, which radiates in his relationships with others....
>
> I need to let you know also about the excellent work accomplished by this volunteer in relation to his sculptures. His work has extended beyond the school, and has received recognition from the City of Nueva Imperial, for which he created a sculpture of a *machi* (indigenous healer), four meters tall, which is soon to be installed at the entrance to the city. With this work to do, our brother will prolong his stay in our country.

Following the inauguration of the sculpture, the Nueva Imperial newspaper reported in Spanish [the English translation is ours]:

> In his work as a Methodist missionary, which he has done for the greater part of his life, we find ourselves in the company of U.S. sculptor Donald White.
>
> He recalls that a great part of his seventy years have been dedicated to sculpting. He has lived with a passion for sculpting, and has taught it in both public and private schools.... He has traveled to fourteen countries in the last fifteen years, leaving in each one examples of his work, whether in wood, marble, or metal.
>
> In these countries, which include Russia, Mexico, and El Salvador, among others, he has taught English, religion, and sculpting. The trips have been financed by his artistic creations....
>
> His educational labor, he says, offers an opportunity to instill values in children by means of art, since "the human spirit needs beautiful things in life."
>
> At this time he is visiting the city as a volunteer, sharing his experience with the students of the Methodist School at La Granja, through classes of modeling in clay. When Mayor Manuel Salas contacted him about the possibility of making a wood statue of a Mapuche, White graciously agreed to take on this task to aid the city's recognition of the Mapuche culture....
>
> The first thing that had to happen in order to see that this work was done was to obtain the trunk of a native tree, which was donated by the Barrera Cansino family. This made it possible for work to begin on the sculpture March 31, when the sculptor hammered the first blows to the wood to begin to shape a four-meter-tall structure....
>
> After two months the sculpture is almost finished, only lacking a few details that White expects to finish by the end of this month, when he will return to his country. The work will be displayed in a place where all can enjoy its beauty.

Volunteering Benefits the Volunteer

Volunteers ask not "What will I get out of it?" but rather "How can I serve others?" Nevertheless, almost all of them find that volunteering has provided rich blessings and unexpected benefits.

Opportunities to serve others lead to spiritual growth. Travel provides new insights into the beauty of God's world. Relating to people of a different culture leads to unforgettable experiences, so that volunteers discover "you receive more than you give."

1. Opportunities to Serve Others

Because the goal of volunteers is to serve others, the opportunity to serve is one of the rewards of volunteering.

Sharon Romich wrote after her first volunteer experience in Nepal:

> I have thoroughly enjoyed my time in Tansen.... I like the rural setting, the United Mission to Nepal community is strong and supportive here, and I have been very needed and appreciated at the Tansen Nursing School. They are at the end of their first year with the new school, and all were ready for the help and support I have been able to give. I have taken the place of one missionary who went on a much-needed home leave, and the two new Nepali nursing faculty have been grateful for my input as they sort out normal problems of beginning a program. It has been very good to feel useful.

Gil Gilman discovered the joy of volunteering in Zimbabwe:

> What am I doing in Africa? I am changing lives! After sixty years of preparation, God has finally put me to work doing his will. When I look into the faces of these children I receive my shower of blessings. I know I am where God wants me to be, doing what he has prepared me to do. I can look around Sakubva and see a million things that need to be done and know I cannot do it all. I don't concentrate on that.... I concentrate on what I can do. I am only lighting one little candle in a vast world of darkness but I know, deeply, that it is better to hold forth my one little candle than to spend a wasted lifetime cursing the darkness.

2. Spiritual Growth

One of the greatest benefits of the volunteer experience is the spiritual enrichment that comes from recognizing that everything depends on God and having to trust completely in the Lord. Volunteers rely on God to help them get through each day in new and unfamiliar surroundings, and God's presence becomes very real as they seek to be faithful servants.

Many of them have told us about experiencing spiritual growth through volunteer service, and we are pleased to share some of their accounts.

The faith and commitment of the Christians in communities where volunteers serve is often an inspiration to the volunteers. **Anita Jackson** wrote in her "Report upon Arrival" after beginning her work in Zimbabwe:

> I thought I would let you know that I am settled here in Zimbabwe and am very much enjoying myself. I have been spending my time at the Old Mutare hospital and am so glad that I get to spend a bit more time here than the Volunteers In Mission teams. It's nice to be able to get to know the nurses and the people here. It is such a blessing to me to be here in so many ways. I've been finding a lot of spiritual challenges and a deep sense of spiritual renewal.

Leon and Doris Graham, volunteers at the Southeastern Jurisdiction's Lake Junaluska Assembly near Asheville, North Carolina, wrote in the November/December 1999 issue of *New World Outlook* magazine about the spiritual side of volunteering:

> The spiritual aspect of individual volunteer work is difficult to describe, but imagine this. You wake up one morning and the whole world seems warm, sunny, and bright. There's a happiness inside you just bursting at the seams to come out. You radiate a feeling of love for everyone you meet. There are no negative thoughts to be found anywhere.
>
> We cannot better describe having had a spiritual experience with our Lord Jesus than by describing the experience of serving him through volunteer services to others. This was his mandate given to us in so many of his teachings, and this is the greatest of all rewards for us as individual volunteers.

Staci Martin, who ran in "adventure races" and marathons in South Africa, reflected on her relationship with Christ:

> The race was worth it. Coming to South Africa was worth it. But what tops these escapades is my "mornings" and "afternoons" with Christ. Some mornings I am filled with excitement and mission. Some afternoons I feel like God is asking me to take the plunge. I am trusting that God's security net is strong enough to hold me.
>
> Other days I have voices, not unlike Roger whispering, "Go at your own pace." And then there are days that I have God carrying my baggage, not unlike Wayne did during the race.... Despite all my shortcomings, I endure because I trust God with all my heart. He hasn't let me down so far.

3. Support from Home and Family

Volunteering usually involves support from home: family, friends, local church (and sometimes the district or the entire annual conference), and the broader community—service clubs, Scouts, schools, and other organizations and individuals. The mission becomes more meaningful as support comes from many different directions.

Julie Meyer wrote from Bolivia:

> Thank you to everyone that sent letters down with my parents. The love and support that you have shown me is overwhelming, and I now have renewed energy for my final months here in Bolivia. Thank you also for the school supplies. You can't imagine what a luxury they are for the students. We are very proud of our "library" in the Tsimane School, and the kids love to have the books read aloud. They also all have their own box of crayons and they take very good care of them....
>
> With the money you sent down, I was able to buy twenty reading books and almost thirty workbooks to practice cursive writing. The reading books focus on themes about the Bolivian countryside (especially the Orient/jungle) so the kids can relate more to them. One of the first activities I had the kids do was read the part on hunting with bows and arrows and then draw and label all the animals they hunt with bow and arrow.

Gil Gilman wrote from Zimbabwe about his experience during a holiday:

> This Christmas is going to be very special for me.... I am going to have the joy of watching forty wonderful kids open their presents on Christmas morning at Fairfield Orphanage....
>
> We have received twice the amount of money we asked for from our supporters in the States. We even had a big donation of toys from one of the merchants in town ... a man who is a devout Muslim. There was a great lesson for many of us in this act of kindness and mercy. When we say, "Peace on earth ... goodwill toward men," let's not say it with blinders on.
>
> Every kid will get what is on his "wish list" and we will have a big Christmas feast. I haven't been this excited about an upcoming Christmas since I was eight years old, tossing and turning in my bed on Christmas Eve, wondering what Santa was going to leave under the Christmas tree. (I guess some of us never grow up ... praise the Lord!)

Another kind of support is receiving visitors from home. Family members or friends who visit are usually well received by the host community, providing further opportunities for forming cross-cultural relationships. Visitors often help with the volunteer's work, or find other ways of serving.

Sharon Romich wrote of her time spent volunteering in Nepal:

> My time in Nepal ended on a very high note, literally and figuratively. Younger daughter Kate and I did a ten-day trek in the Annapurna sanctuary. What a beautiful way to end. We flew into Jomson at 2,700 meters, hiked up to Muktinath, a sacred place for both Buddhists and Hindus at 3,800 meters, and then slowly made our way down the trail.
>
> The trek starts in the high, dry, isolated country close to Tibet and then goes south through pine forests and hills until it gets to the low hills with rice fields and semitropical jungles. All this is between Dhaulagiri, the Himal, which is the eighth-highest mountain in the world, and Annapurna I, the eleventh-highest. Spectacular scenery and interesting cultures and people along the way.

Nicole Windhurst wrote about her brother's visit to Zimbabwe:

This month we will begin cutting down the dry eight-foot stalks of maize in our 200-meter by 100-meter field and making way for the foundations of eight two-unit homes that we hope will be ready for the children by the end of the year. My brother, Louis, has come for two months to consult on the building project, work on a play structure for the kids, and keep me sane during some of the more trying times around here.

The other day I went to check on Lou as he was repairing one of the four broken washing machines at the orphanage. A whirlwind descended upon us and hit us with the force of a mini-tornado. Dust and toys go flying up in the air, carpets are pulled up from the floor, doors and windows slam, and many nerves are rattled. We hear glass shatter—nearly all the windowpanes have been busted out over the years, and as we turn around we see the last remaining panel in the laundry room crash to the floor. It is time to move out of this building.

However, **Jack and Judy Schaible**, who volunteered in Chile, learned that it is not always wise to indiscriminately invite friends from home to visit. They wrote to the congregation Jack had served as a pastor in Arkansas prior to retiring:

Well, I'm humbled because when I invited all of you, never did I believe that you would come. I guess I got a little carried away in describing our wonderful rental in Chile. It does have a view of the ocean. That part was true. But it is a wee bit smaller than the way I described. There really isn't any room for Judy and me, plus guests, to sleep in our rental. But if you will still come, I promise you, we will give you the bedroom with the ocean view and we will sleep on the lower level. If after you open the attachment to this e-mail you still want to come, we will welcome you with open arms.

4. Relationships with People of a Different Culture

Probably the most vital part of the volunteer experience is the lasting relationships formed between long-term volunteers and the friends they make in the places where they serve. It has been a continuing source of joy to receive reports like the ones that follow.

Cally Curtis wrote of her friends in Belize:

> The people here are quite taken aback by my being here alone. It just doesn't register in this nation of extended family. And I'm thankful that they have gathered me in, like part of the harvest. I'm always welcomed with warm smiles, a gentle hand on my shoulder as someone passes, a shout and waved hello from someone driving by in their car.

Dr. **Nelson Bailey**, volunteering in Palestine, commented: "My personal relationships with the Palestinian Christians have created a lifelong union. They demonstrated to me that we are indeed of one flock under a single omnipotent Lord."

Having established deeply affectionate relationships, saying goodbye can be emotionally wrenching.

The Reverend **Leta Gorham** wrote of leaving Nepal:

> As the plane started down the runway, I caught a final glimpse of the faces of the people I had loved so quickly and so deeply. The plane climbed into the sky and moved out and away from the place I had called home for a year—the Top of the World. Those special mountains that had brought me so much beauty and stillness in my soul were there for another moment of peace. "Thank you, loving God, for so many blessings," I whispered. Tears of joy filled my heart and my eyes as I tried to say, "*Pheri bhe taulaa*," "Au revoir," "Until we meet again."

Staci Martin, a volunteer in South Africa, wrote:

> Nothing prepared me for this. Nothing. I have only known the group of youngsters for ten weeks. And I suppose a lot can happen in a matter of weeks. I have seen about 250 children and youth throughout the year and a half I have been in South Africa. I have had children cope in different ways regarding the ending of the ten-week program,

what we call in therapy land the dreaded "T" word—*Termination*. Sure, I was prepared for my children and youth to be upset, sad and confused, but nothing prepared me for what I was about to witness.

I had children break down and cry. Not one but several. I allowed them to cry as long as they needed to. Holding their hands. I wanted to scoop them in my lap, but knew if I did that I would have all six children wanting the same. I knew what they were crying about had nothing to do with the program and in the same breath had everything to do with the program. It affirmed that what I was doing here in South Africa was worthwhile, appreciated, and used.

On the flip side, I had children telling me that I couldn't leave. I had invites for me to live with them in their homes. And then I had the most unexpected thing happen to me. This group was never difficult. In fact they were the most compliant group I worked with in the year and a half. We were finishing up, and I went through my routine. I am not very good at this "ending thing." So most of the time, out of self-preservation, I go on automatic pilot.

They sat around the table with their little smiling faces, bums glued to their chairs, determined not to leave. It was a "happy revolt." It was painful each time I said they could leave. They smiled. Quietly spoke to one another in their language. They did not move. Then one had to go to the bathroom. Charity left. She returned. They smiled, and I asked, "How long are we going to sit here?" Tskani chimed in Xhosa. Another classmate interpreted, "She will be eating and sleeping here."

Forty-five minutes later, the revolt ended when the teacher asked them to return to their class. I was stunned, attempting to comprehend what had just taken place. Throw out the theory and practice books. I did the termination process by the book. But this time it didn't work.

5. Travel and New Insights into the Beauty of God's World

Although the purpose of volunteering is to meet the needs of churches and institutions that cannot afford enough paid staff to fulfill all of their goals for serving the people of the host community, volunteers are usually people who love to travel and want to see other parts of the country, or of the world, from the perspective of the people who live there rather than from the perspective of the ordinary tourist. Living in another country, or another part of one's own country, can facilitate exploring nearby tourist attractions and traveling to neighboring countries.

Local people are usually eager for volunteers to see interesting and beautiful sites in their part of the world, whether it be visiting Mayan ruins in Central America, climbing mountains and volcanoes, participating in festivals, seeing historic places, or going on a safari to get acquainted with native wildlife.

Rob and Pam Porter said of their time in Ghana: "The adventures to see the elephants, warthogs, antelope, crocodiles, and monkey colonies were exciting (and made it all worth while). Walking on suspended 'bridges' one hundred feet up in the air in a rain forest was frosting on the cake."

Steve Paylor wrote about Chile:

> I went to the Conguillio National Park with Claudio and Rodrigo, friends from town. It wasn't a bad drive, but nearly all on two-lane roads, sometimes gravel. The drive in the park started out as a primitive but smooth road through the assorted volcanic rock left over from the eruption of *Volcán Llaima* (Llaima Volcano) in 1957. The landscape was all black from this eruption, with trees poking out from the rubble and a few lakes. One was especially eerie with green colors underwater and trees visible at the bottom.
>
> We parked the car and started a hike for a few hours up one of the mountains. That was an incredible hike: the landscape was varied from forest to volcanic rock, and the forest was all native Chilean plants, a marked difference from the imported trees that are now all that is seen in most of the region. . . .
>
> There were waterfalls coming from the snow at the top of the mountains, and we had a chance to refill our water bottles from one of the streams. We retraced our steps back down the trail and went swimming at a beach at a nearby (cold) lake, and then drove out of the park a different way. This route went through some of the old forest and I could get a feel for what the country would have looked like before. Tall, tall trees in a mature spacing dimming the light from sun above, make one think about the old forests in *The Lord of the Rings*.
>
> I felt really good about seeing this park. Pablo Neruda said that

"anyone who hasn't been in the Chilean forest doesn't know this planet," and that's about what I would expect from a state poet, but having been to the park, I feel like I have been to the natural Chile that people come here to see.

Being away from home seems to open our eyes to the beauty of the natural world as we encounter scenery that is different from what we are accustomed to seeing every day. Many volunteers have written very poetically about the beauty around them, as in the examples below. **Nicole Windhurst** wrote about Zimbabwe:

It was the type of sunset that makes postcard photographers crazy. Wisps of clouds lay low between descending layers of mountains— each cloud a complementary shade of pink, orange, red, and purple. Everything had a glowing silver lining and between two of the mountains the last piece of the sun poked through and you could follow each ray across the farm valley. Intense shades of violet and fuchsia were everywhere....

Fall is in full swing, and the trees are turning their own shades of red and orange interspersed with the bright evergreen pines. As I drive over the windy mountain pass that divides "town" from the rural valley I call home, I am simultaneously in Vermont and Hawaii and overwhelmed to the point where I am forced to pull over the car and catch my own breath. God is truly in this place.

Sharon Romich described Nepal this way:

The countryside around Tansen is absolutely gorgeous now, green and lush.... The rice fields are beginning to be planted. They start with a patch of very thick plants, which is the seed bed. Then they prepare the rest of the fields, mostly plowing with buffalo and breaking up clods of dirt with hand tools. Then they flood the field, and groups of people take the rice seedlings and transplant them in the field in rows about four inches apart. The planters are usually women who work in a long line moving across the fields.... Sometimes you can hear them sing as they plant. It is a happy time, as the rice is such a significant part of their life and culture.

Becky Harrell, a volunteer in Chile, wrote about her time there:

> Springtime in Chile. Not just spring in Chile, but spring in Chile in the desert. Not just spring in Chile in the desert, but spring in Chile in the desert with color. Lots of color. Bougainvilleas are about the hottest pinks and reddest reds I have ever seen. The hibiscus are large, full plants with such variations of color; the most popular appear to be peach. Who would have ever thought that a city in the desert could be so beautiful? . . .
>
> Music; along with spring comes music of God's creation. Each morning, about 6:00 a.m., I have the pleasure of listening to a symphony before raising my head from the pillow. There is a mourning dove whose coo is mellow and a thousand birds whose singing blends harmoniously. It is a sound that brings a smile to your face and brushes the sleep from your eyes, giving you the first glimpse of what is sure to be a glorious day.

6. Unforgettable Experiences

Some volunteer experiences are unique and cannot be easily categorized, so we are simply presenting a variety of remarkable adventures recounted by individual volunteers. Some are difficult and devastating, others enjoyable and uplifting, but all are representative of the kinds of things that happen when individual volunteers immerse themselves in the communities they serve.

The Reverend **Leta Gorham**, who went to Nepal as a pastoral counselor for the missionary community, described one of the conditions she encountered there:

> "She gave birth to her first son, wrapped him in cloths and laid him in a manger—there was *no room* for them to stay in the inn." We have read this story many times, put on our bathrobes, located a cane or two, even had a live cow or sheep in the scene. We know that it is a story of another age—at least two thousand years ago. But, do we realize how hard that must have been for Mary?
>
> I now live in a country where that story is lived out every day, and it is the year 2000. For in the western part of Nepal there is a region

with little health awareness, and tradition says that women in labor must go to the cow shed to give birth to avoid the gods' anger if they delivered in the home. After delivery, they must stay in the cow shed for twenty days eating a prescribed diet. This practice contributes to a very high infant and maternal mortality rate.

There is hope. United Mission to Nepal has two auxiliary nurse midwives in that area who give as much care as possible to the mother and child and work to move the baby "out of the manger" and into the home.

Nicole Windhurst decided to adopt Tsitsi, one of the AIDS orphans she worked with at Fairfield Children's Home in Zimbabwe. She described her first encounter with Tsitsi:

Her little head of unkempt hair lay awkwardly on the small, child-size table in the middle of the hospital children's ward. Her clothes were obviously borrowed—the natty bathrobe was meant for a full-size adult and was so worn that you could stick your fist through dozens of the holes. A woman's T-shirt, which was probably once white, was now a dingy yellowy gray and long enough for her to use as a dress. Tsitsi apathetically stares out the window and passes away the hours. Her bare feet shuffle between cots of coughing, bleeding, bandaged children looking for the tiniest piece of kindness.

Tsitsi was three and a half years old when her mother passed away, and her father had died just a year before that. Social Welfare had refused to take custody of her, because she had one living relative left—a young, single aunt who was not thrilled about taking in the little toddler. Within a few months, her aunt found herself pregnant and faced with the prospect of feeding another mouth. Two days after her delivery, she wrapped up her newborn and slipped out the doors of Mutare Provincial Hospital, leaving four-and-a-half-year-old Tsitsi alone and abandoned again. . . .

Tsitsi does not adjust to the new situation well. Though she never causes problems, she can't quite fit in to the hectic atmosphere of the orphanage. The children here have grown up together from infancy, and have a very close-knit bond that is hard to break into. Tsitsi spends her days quietly unhappy. . . . The construction project is coming along well and we expect the first homes to be completed in a matter of weeks. I request that Tsitsi stay with me until the first home is done and she can transition into a quieter, less-chaotic atmosphere.

At my home, Tsitsi comes alive. She is a little chatterbox, singing nonsensical songs and playing dress-up with her dolls. Her face is full of light and joy—an unrecognizable creature compared to what I saw in the hospital those first days. She is affectionate, charming, and beautiful. Tsitsi has been taught impeccable manners—she bathes and brushes her teeth meticulously, and eats carefully, using both African and European manners....

Sunday night (August 18) I am waiting for my parents to call. It has been a long day of cooking, cleaning, and doing laundry by hand. I am exhausted but still excited to talk to my family. I have absolutely loved the last month of having Tsitsi stay with me, and she has become, in my mind, my little girl. I have long debated the pros and cons of adoption as a twenty-five-year-old single parent, but with this little girl there was no question. Now I was just waiting to begin a realistic discussion with my parents.

Sunday night comes and goes, and no phone call. With the unpredictability of the phone lines here, this is not terribly shocking, and I know they will try to call again the next evening. An epidemic of chicken pox has been going around the orphanage, and we have forty-seven children, none of whom have ever been exposed or had the vaccine (we are stocking up on calamine lotion and saying our prayers). Tsitsi was one of the first to start showing spots, so in addition to playing Mommy, I also get to play Nurse Niko as well. Tsitsi's case was pretty bad, and she sleeps little at night.

The next morning the painkillers have finally kicked in and she is able to rest. I take advantage of a few hours to myself and leave her sleeping with my roommate while I run to town to do some errands, including picking up a copy of the international adoption regulations.

My friend tells me that Tsitsi has refused to eat, and is starting to run a temperature. I take her down to the hospital and wait to see the doctor to ask what else can be done. Dr. Manyeza hands me a letter from Lab Services—Tsitsi is HIV-positive, and unlikely to survive the chicken pox. We put her on a new injection series, painkillers, and Gentian Violet for the pox in her mouth and throat. She is on nine different medications and a host of different vitamins.

In forty-eight hours I watch my little girl deteriorate to a state of illness that is painful to watch in such a beautiful child. She is itching and uncomfortable all the time, and she is covered in millions of sores. At one count, she had nearly thirty blisters just on the palm of one tiny hand. Tuesday was the worst day, with her fever peaking at 105.1°F. She looks at me with these pleading eyes, begging me to make it all better, and I know there is very little I can do.

Tuesday afternoon her symptoms relax. There is nothing more the hospital can do, and she has been begging to go "home" all day. The nurses agree to discharge her since her temperature is now normal, and she even agrees to let me carry her the half mile to my house, though I know it rubs on her millions of sores. She is again playful, affectionate, and lively. The joy has returned to her eyes, and I see my little angel again. I did not know it at the time, but this was my last chance to say good-bye.

While cleaning up the dinner dishes, I hear from the next room the terrible sound of a child vomiting. Tsitsi throws up everything she has eaten, all the water she drank, and all the medicines she had that day. Her body is finished with all of it. Her teeth start chattering, and though it is warm outside, her temperature is 95.1°F. I wrap her in her favorite blanket and start running for the hospital. Nurses attempt oxygen and an IV, but her delusions cause her to fight all of it.... The seizures are too much for her; she turns to look at me, reaches out her arm, and suddenly is gone....

The house, and my life, has a certain emptiness. I still expect her to come running out of the house to meet me and wake up early in the morning expecting to be pounced on. I am comforted that she is in heaven with her biological family, happy to be reunited with her mom and dad. Her suffering is over. I have spent the last days trying to calm and comfort her suffering and pain, and now it is her turn to look down on me and comfort me as I try to move on without her....

I am exhausted, physically and emotionally.... I am so grateful for the mission community; everyone has been very sympathetic and compassionate. Many, many people have come to offer condolences. In the few months that Tsitsi stayed with us, she was a light and an inspiration in this community that loved her very much. I cannot possibly express how much I will miss her, or how much she meant in my life....

In forty-eight hours I went from thinking about which university Tsitsi might attend to picking out an outfit for her to be buried in. There is no torture ever invented that could compare to losing a child.... I cannot imagine the pain of millions of families in southern Africa going through the same situation, most of whom don't have the resources to offer painkillers and antibiotics to their little ones. AIDS is an unmerciful thief, and no family in Zimbabwe goes untouched. Tsitsi fought the HIV virus until the very last second.... I pray that we can learn from Tsitsi's courage to fight this disease that kills millions of adults and children every year.

Fortunately, most experiences volunteers write about are happier ones, such as the following.
Sharon Romich wrote from Nepal:

I was wakened this morning at 6:25 a.m. by a very enthusiastic knock on the door. First, I had to find something to put on, as answering the door in one's nightgown, no matter how long it is, is not an option in Nepal. Dr. Rachel was asleep upstairs, probably with her earplugs in, as she was trying to recover from a horrendous night on call and trying to catch up on her sleep. So I went to the door to find a woman who began talking in rapid-fire Nepali. I figured out she was a census taker and I was about to be included in the official 2001 Nepali census. This is great irony, as I missed the 2000 U.S. census!

Of course, I could not understand her and told her so in my pidgin Nepali. Then she asked for my name, which I had to spell very slowly in English for her. She kept asking me how many people lived here, and I kept telling her two. But she didn't believe me. It is pretty unbelievable in Nepal that only two people would live in a ten-room house. But she kept asking, "How many people?" and I kept saying "two." Finally I gave her Rachel's name and added "Dr.," so I think she figured it out. She did not ask any other questions, like age, nationality, residence status, etc. It must have been just a nose count. So much for a quiet sleep-in on my only day off in the week.

On another occasion, Sharon was privileged to attend a very special event:

What a day yesterday was! I arrived at the nursing campus at 8:00 a.m., and of course I was one of the first people there. Soon after everyone arrived, Mr. Sharma, the older man who works in the office, came to deliver invitations that Bishnu had left for anyone who wanted to go to the opening of the Fourteenth Asian Conference on Mental Retardation downtown at the Royal Academy at 11:00 a.m. The big draw was that the queen, Her Royal Highness, was going to do the inauguration....

We arrived at the Royal Academy at 11:05 a.m., even though our invitation said no one would be admitted after 11:00 a.m., and we were quite concerned that we had missed the queen's grand entrance. No, the queen's planners were smart; she was not scheduled to arrive until 11:30 a.m. They knew you had to tell Nepalese an earlier time if you had any hope of starting on time....

The queen finally arrived at 11:45 a.m. and the conference got started.... The queen said nothing; she just sat on a couch covered by a fancy red blanket with lots of glitter on it. Rhadia commented that they think their queen is "beautiful even though she is a little plump." She has beautiful skin. It is light and flawless in a country where many people show damage from the sun. She was dressed in an elaborate yellow *sari* (Indian dress). There was a little ceremony in which the program was presented to her with a big red ribbon tied around it, and to the rest of the dignitaries on the stage. Ganga, a member of our faculty, was one of two people onstage presenting programs. Then the queen walked over to a little Hindu shrine onstage and lit the ceremonial butter lamp and the conference got started.

I was most impressed with several things. First, there was this conference and hence concern about mental retardation in Asia. They had a group of people from a sheltered workshop dressed in beautiful native costumes sing a song at the beginning. Some of them were quite disabled; they had to be led onto the stage and kept in place by gentle nudges from behind.

One of the keynote speakers was disabled. He told his story about how his life was nothing until the British doctors at Shanta Bhanwan, the old United Mission to Nepal hospital before Patan hospital, helped his parents with his care. He now has a job as a teacher's aide in a sheltered workshop. His speech was in Nepali and then was interpreted into English. I will say he was the one speaker for whom the queen actually turned her head and listened.

Jim Kersey, while he was volunteering in India, wrote the following:

This past weekend, I took part in a Student Leadership Retreat. We took forty-three students from Woodstock School down into a Christian Retreat Center in Dehra Dun (about twenty-one miles *down* the mountain—the bus trip down and up was an adventure in itself). . . . I and another fellow took fourteen students to the Shady Side School.

That was all I knew until I got to the front gate, which read: "Shady Side School for Blind Girls." A fascinating and moving experience. One of the important factors to understand is the role of females in most of Indian society. The birth of a female is not always celebrated. As the director told me, most of these girls would have been abandoned, if even permitted to live, if not for this institution. Here they will be taught how to read Braille and taught skills to survive in the larger world.

At first our students were very hesitant. I remember especially one young girl from Australia who was just standing around after most of the others had gone off with some of the blind children. I went over to her and asked what made her feel most uncomfortable—the cultural differences or their blindness. She said, "I don't speak Hindi, so what can I say or do that would mean anything?"

In the meantime, there was a blind girl just standing by herself looking very lost. I encouraged the Aussie to try. Reluctantly, she approached the blind girl and took her hand. The smile on the face of the blind girl, just by the human touch, I will never forget. Language became not necessary for these two girls. I did get one of our Hindi-speaking girls to come and translate between the two girls for a few minutes. By the end of our stay, these two frightened humans, who could not verbally communicate, had forged a meaningful relationship. God's grace was there.

7. Discovering That "You Receive Much More Than You Give"

One thread that runs through the correspondence we have received from volunteers is the recognition that being a volunteer brings many blessings, so that the rewards of volunteering far outweigh any drawbacks.

Pamela Karg wrote of her time in Armenia: "I returned forty-eight hours ago from my six weeks of volunteering with UMCOR in

Armenia. I *loved it*! In fact, God saw to it that the whole experience touched the very core of my soul. It has been the most powerful experience of my life."

Irene Mparutsa, who volunteered in Cambodia and now serves as a missionary there, wrote:

> I have come to realize that you give so much and you get back much more than you could ever dream. I am growing in my faith as I witness; the love, care, and friendship that I receive from strangers as well as from people of faith is teaching me invaluable lessons; not having all the answers to the host of problems we encounter daily has helped me stay close to him who is able. It is a big challenge, yes, yet I sense fulfillment.

6

After the Volunteer Experience

*Some of the volunteers are considering returning to their places of
service for another time of volunteering. Others have decided to enter
the full-time pastoral ministry. All have been transformed by their
mission experience, and recommend the experience for all young
adults who want to deepen their faith, begin to understand some of the
justice issues facing the world today, and be in ministry with God's
people in a different cultural setting from their own.*
—FROM A NEWS ARTICLE ABOUT THE "AÑO VOLUNTARIO"
(YEAR OF VOLUNTEERING) SPONSORED BY THE YOUTH
OF THE METHODIST CHURCH OF CHILE

*M*ost volunteers upon returning home find that their lives
have been profoundly changed. They may find it hard to
readjust to life in their home country, and their families
may find them a bit hard to get along with at first. **Jackie Fagin** of
Villa Park, Illinois, spoke to past and future individual volunteers at
a combined orientation/training and individual volunteer reunion in
August 2004 about what it is like to be the spouse of a recently

returned volunteer. She began by saying that when a volunteer first comes home, he or she is likely to be an obnoxious person. The only thing volunteers want to talk about at first is the place where they have been, the people they have met, and the experiences they have had.

Jackie said when her husband, **Bo**, returned from Senegal after his first volunteer experience, she would say, "Bo, would you please take out the garbage?" and he would reply with "That reminds me of a time in Senegal...," and off he would go with another story, forgetting about the request she had made. So when Bo volunteered a second time in Senegal, Jackie decided to meet him in Paris on his way home. As they walked down the Champs Élysées, Bo spotted a McDonald's, and he grabbed her hand and ran as fast as he could to get a hamburger. "And he doesn't even like McDonald's hamburgers back in the States," she concluded.

Some volunteers have definite plans already lined up before they head for home. A frequently asked question, however, is, "What do I do now?" Volunteers often find the culture shock more acute upon returning home than when they arrived at their place of service.

Reentry Stress and Adjustment

Reentry stress (reverse culture shock) is manifested in feelings of disorientation and being out of place, feeling disillusioned, being irritated with others and with certain aspects of one's own culture, or feeling lonely, isolated, depressed, and misunderstood.

To lessen the impact of reverse culture shock, it is wise for volunteers to be prepared to deal with the stress of reentry. During the orientation/training, and in the Individual Volunteer Handbook, volunteers are given suggestions for things they can do before leaving for home, and after arriving at home, to help them readjust to life in their home country, in spite of the changes that have taken place in their lives due to the impact of the volunteer experience.

The stages of reverse culture shock are similar to those of culture shock. L. Robert Kohls, in the *Survival Kit for Overseas Living*, lists the four stages of the adjustment process as initial euphoria, irritability and hostility, gradual adjustment, and adaptation or biculturalism.

Stage 1: Initial Euphoria

It is so good to be back in well-known surroundings, hearing one's native tongue spoken with a familiar accent, eating favorite foods, and visiting favorite places, that at first everything seems wonderful. **Howard Pisons and Cheryl Lafferty** wrote after their return from Chile:

> So the Chile adventure is over. One year went by way too fast! We've unpacked and are trying to remember where we put things one year ago. Rebecca, who was staying in our house while we were gone, has left now for a fantastic new opportunity in Wisconsin. And our house is cleaner now than when we lived here. We are really going to miss her. This was a perfect example of how God uses us to help each other.

Stage 2: Irritability and Hostility

Irritability and hostility are often symptoms of homesickness for the place left behind, but they also may be caused by disappointment with the perceived lack of interest on the part of family, friends, and even fellow church members, in learning all about the volunteer's life-changing experiences. Another factor is likely to be disillusionment with the materialism and consumerism of United States society when compared with the lifestyle the volunteer has experienced in another country. **Sharon Romich** wrote after being in Nepal:

> I am having lots of trouble getting used to life back here at home after this second time in Nepal. . . . Life is now so uncertain here in the United States [after the events of September 11, 2001, which occurred as Sharon was en route home from Nepal].

167

I went to a wedding of a son of a friend yesterday, and it all seemed unreal. It was a fancy American wedding and such a huge contrast to the poverty and scarcity in Nepal. I can't get the image of the last burned child in Tansen out of my mind. He was a beautiful three-month-old who "rolled into the fire" in the middle of the night. . . . And being in the middle of all the affluence and modernity of the U.S. doesn't seem to help.

I guess I am just in the middle of conflicting emotions. There is huge relief to be home safely, back on United States soil. And there is sharp realization of how much my family and friends, especially my eighty-four-year-old parents, who have gotten more frail even in three months, are also hugely relieved to have me safely home. All this is contrasted with the memories of the dear friends I left in Tansen and the big need for nursing instructors there to get the fledgling new nursing school on its feet. Not to mention jet lag from trying to switch from a twelve-hour difference in time zones.

Stage 3: Gradual Adjustment

Volunteers may find upon returning home that there have been major changes in the volunteer's family that require a time of adjustment. Also, volunteers may find themselves moving from being concerned primarily with spiritual matters to being concerned primarily with practical matters; from being surrounded with Christian encouragement and fellowship to being with other Christians only on Sunday morning and Wednesday evening; from seeing poverty first-hand to experiencing seemingly overwhelming wealth; from being somebody special to feeling like a nobody.

Carolyn Pesheck wrote after returning from Kenya:

So far, I haven't had any trouble adjusting to life back in the United States, and have been very gratified with the number of questions I've gotten from all sorts of people (many that I didn't know were even aware of what I did). I was interviewed for an internal communication at work, was given a small "reward" for asking my company to donate some equipment to the hospital, and generally feel that people think what I did was rather extraordinary. Much more than I think it was! I've pretty well sorted out the financial side of things here, didn't have any disasters with my house or anything while I was gone, so I feel pretty good about things. I feel very supported here in my adjustment back into the United States.

Stage 4: Adaptation and Biculturalism

Volunteers often realize that they cannot maintain the same lifestyle patterns, relationships, and habits that made up their lives before their mission experience. How do they deal with their emotions? How do they keep from appearing elitist to their friends? How do they adjust to a new value system? How do they bring their new commitment to mission to all they are and do as Christian disciples?

Steve Paylor wrote after returning from Chile: "Things are pretty good. I had some culture shock but seem to be okay now. Although I thought my time in Chile was sort of a lump-sum giving, I find myself still dissatisfied with the rat race. I plan to explore social work but probably will teach (in a bad Philadelphia school) in a year or two."

Continuing the Mission

Many volunteers continue the work they have begun by staying on longer than they had planned, volunteering repeatedly in the same location, volunteering in other places, becoming a commissioned missionary of the General Board of Global Ministries, or continuing the work from home. As a pastor said when introducing **Leta Gorham** to his congregation, "Leta may retire, but she will never retire from Mission."

1. Staying Longer than Planned

Gil Gilman, who went to Zimbabwe to teach history for one year at Africa University, spent several years at the university and later worked with orphanages and schools in Zimbabwe. We met **Jasmine**

Miller, who was already a longtime volunteer at McCurdy School in New Mexico, at a Volunteers In Mission rally in Oklahoma and arranged for her to be a part of the Individual Volunteer program. Reverend **Joyce Mauler Michael**, who went to the Czech Republic to work with The United Methodist Church there and later joined the Individual Volunteer program, continues to volunteer in the Czech Republic and is now married to a Presbyterian missionary. **Larry Cox** has been a volunteer in Matamoros, Mexico, since 2002. These are only a few of those who have stayed on for long periods of time. Some others are quoted below.

Janine Roberts wrote from Zimbabwe, where she continued to serve for several years after first going there:

> I continue to live in Zimbabwe ... and work with the outreach program Project HOPE as well as with the children at Fairfield Children's Home. I am hoping that by the end of this year, the HOPE programs will be turned over to Zimbabwean men and women who have worked so hard for the orphaned and HIV-positive community.

Diane Walrath wrote from North Carolina:

> Here at MERCI we are just getting into the rebuilding in the aftermath of Hurricane Isabel, and I realize it's going to take longer ... to do this. There are still a lot of people without homes or who are living in damaged homes. So after a lot of prayer, I have decided to stay here at MERCI longer than I originally anticipated.

2. Volunteering Again—and Again

Sharon Romich served twice in Nepal, teaching nursing at Tansen Hospital. **Jack and Judy Schaible** spend approximately half of each year volunteering in Chile. **Morris and Ann Taber**, who planned to be in Zimbabwe for one semester, have returned almost every year for at least a short visit. **Chuck Wheat** spends every summer, and sometimes a few months in the winter, hosting Volunteers In Mission teams in Costa Rica. Many others have found a way to return to their places of service, including the following.

Karen Pienkos wrote after her second time in Kentucky:

> I was at the Bennett Center of London for about five wonderful weeks this summer. I worked with some of the same people as I did last year, but many new people also. I worked ten hours a day, five days a week, with the Christian day camp for kids ages four to eleven. The day camp was run by about seven volunteers, and we worked together beautifully. The camp had about forty kids, so we were quite busy (arts and crafts, Bible lessons, pottery, recreation, praise and worship singing, nature lesson, etc.).
>
> God gave me strength to have patience with the kids every day. I was able to see God in each of them through their stories of hard home life, and through the affection and attention they longed for. I hope I was able to plant a mustard seed of faith in the kids that one day they will be able to similarly help others in the community through the Lord's strength and guidance.
>
> I was able to really bond with the other volunteers, some close in age with me, and some farther. They were truly a living presence of God to me each day, which was an amazing blessing at this time in my life. They challenged me daily to become more of a witness, and through them, I grew as a Christian. An experience like that stays with you always. I am so thankful God led me to Kentucky again.

Pamela Karg wrote from Armenia in January 2007:

> Since my initial six weeks here in 2004, I returned in 2005 for six months but stayed seven months. I went home this past April, May, and June to close out many aspects of my life there. I returned to Armenia and UMCOR June 28, 2006, and I don't have a return ticket to America. *That's* how much this experience touched my soul. I feel this is the place and the time when God wants me to serve in this way. So I'll remain until... well, ultimately until he puts something else in my heart.
>
> My duties here remain much as they were in 2004—helping with PR/communications, editing, writing, photography, and helping people with English. I also do a lot of research to try to find potential grants/donors....

171

In addition to all of this, I teach at the Agribusiness Teaching Center, a department of the Armenian Agricultural University that is sponsored by the U.S. Department of Agriculture and Texas A & M. It seems like a lot, but it's really not...and when my heart is so filled with joy, nothing seems too insurmountable with God's guiding hand!

3. Volunteering in Other Places

Whether within the United States or in a variety of other countries, many volunteers find that one time of volunteering is not enough. They seek out opportunities to learn about new places and meet new people, and to be of service wherever God leads them.

Dr. **Nelson Bailey**, an oral surgeon, probably holds the record for volunteering in the greatest number of countries with a number of medical volunteer organizations. Reverend **Leta Gorham**, a former missionary, has volunteered in the Democratic Republic of the Congo, Nepal, and Korea. **Don White** has served in Russia, El Salvador, Palestine, and at two locations in Chile.

Reverend **Robert Paulen** wrote several years after his first volunteer assignment in the Bahamas:

> Two years ago I served in a local church as an English tutor in the Czech Republic. Last winter I split my time between Costa Rica where I assisted a seminary librarian and Belize where I hosted Volunteers In Mission teams.... Next year I hope to take another individual VIM assignment.

Diane Walrath, currently a staff member at the Midwest Mission Distribution Center, Chatham, Illinois, began her volunteer work in Puebla, Mexico, and later served at MERCI (Marion Edwards Recovery Center Initiatives), Goldsboro, North Carolina.

Judith Richerzhagen, after going to Kenya Methodist University as an individual volunteer, found another place in Africa for volunteer service:

God kept calling me back to Africa. . . . In the fall of 2006 I went as a voluntary nursing tutor for the University of Livingstonia, Ekwendeni Campus. It was an awesome experience. My clinical skills and insights were welcomed and solicited by both teachers and nurses at the attached hospital. That work was in a mission sponsored by the Presbyterian Church. I smile as my mission work was supported by my two congregations here, St. Luke's Episcopal Church and Grace Lutheran, ELCA. God clearly doesn't let denominational divisions stand in the way of his work. . . .

The two students who were with me were there for three weeks; then I began to spend full time with the college and hospital. Malawi describes itself as the warm heart of Africa. Clearly, my care and acceptance by those in charge was gracious and thoughtful. I also made many friends while in Malawi with folks there. The transition to another culture was, of course, aided by my previous time in Africa.

I am home again, waiting on the Lord for his next assignment.

Jane Boone, who began volunteering at age seventy-four, served at Scarritt-Bennett Center, Nashville, Tennessee; Heifer Ranch in Perryville, Arkansas; and Cook College, Tempe, Arizona. Other United States volunteers have later ventured farther abroad.

Dave and Jan Calley have volunteered both in the United States and in Ghana:

We have been active with NOMADS projects in the United States since completing our year at Midwest Mission Distribution Center. Last fall we had the joy of delivering a fire truck from an Illinois fire department to the United Methodist Camp on the Boulder at Big Timber, Montana, right in the midst of the forest fires in the area.

During our year at MMDC we made three shipments to Ghana for a Ghana native who is an oncologist in Springfield, Illinois. Through his nonprofit organization he has been able to provide medical and other aid in his home country. After shipping farm machinery he wanted us to go and help teach the use of the machinery. So we made a trip to Ghana for that, and Jan also helped with the patients that Dr. Agamah treated.

173

Allie Miller first volunteered at McCurdy School in Espanola, New Mexico; later went with a mission organization to Zambia; and then was a ministry intern at Horizons International, a mission organization in Boulder, Colorado. She wrote shortly before her departure for Zambia:

> I'm blessed to have you partnering with me on this journey!
> We are leaving July 17 (nineteen days away as I type this letter). Praise God that there is still time for us to grow and prepare. *Preparation* is a word that we have spoken of a lot lately. Prepare for what? To experience God in a new way, as he reveals himself in Zambia— through the people, the culture, the country, the churches, the worship.
> Once again I'll tell you that we need you on the team.
> 1. By thanking God for his gifts (James 1:17). Our tickets are bought. We have four more meetings scheduled. We have been blessed by support from our friends and family. God has spoken to us individually and collectively. Jesus is interceding for us (Hebrews 7:25).
> 2. Encouragement letters. This is one way that I really hope you can support me during my time in Zambia. I would *love* to have a letter (or two or five or ten) to open from you! (Reference Acts 15:30-31.) I know there will be times when I feel tired, worn out, discouraged, and empty. How God will speak to me through his Word and through other people's encouragement during this time! ... You can mail (or e-mail) the letters to me in the next three weeks, and just write Zambia somewhere on the envelope so that I know not to open it yet! ...
> 3. Financial support. Please remember this is only one form of support, but an important one. I am still praying to God for $500 to cover the cost of our plane ticket ($2,100), food, other travel expenses, Bibles to share, and our group donation to the mission in Zambia. I am trusting God that he will provide.

Some volunteers continue their individual volunteer service while also joining volunteer teams from time to time. **Frank and Mary Hedgcock** have not only returned to Bolivia, taking teams with them, but have also served in other locations, including the Czech Republic. **Tom and Nancy Hyle**, in addition to Tom's volunteer service in China, have served on teams in Huancayo, Peru, and Maua, Kenya.

Former volunteers often become volunteers in their own communities. **Jeanie Pennington,** returning from the Czech Republic, wrote to us about her volunteer work, both locally and through Volunteers In Mission:

> I have done some volunteering locally with my church—painting the outside of a Methodist church in Pilger, painting the interior of a new Methodist church in Hallam (after a tornado demolished their previous structure).... I also participated in a VIM experience in Honduras last January—yet another wonderful experience, which ended with my crying because I didn't want to leave....
>
> I have become active in United Methodist Women—as you suggested. This year I am the Education and Interpretation Coordinator for our unit and devotional leader for our circle. Yes, I am enjoying it, as you knew I would. Also keeping me busy is participating on our contemporary service planning committee and chairing our ministry planning team. *And,* I've been talked into (once again, I couldn't think of a good reason to say no to God) chairing our church council. Yes, it has been a busy few months.

Jeanie's mission experience inspired her daughter to become a missionary through the US-2 program of the General Board of Global Ministries, in which young people serve in mission settings in the United States for two years: "Our daughter is a US-2 missionary at Cunningham Children's School in Urbana, Illinois. When you shared with me about US-2's, I took that information home to her, and, *voilá!*"

4. Becoming a Career Missionary

Some former volunteers who have become commissioned missionaries of the United Methodist General Board of Global Ministries are **John Elmore, Becky Harrell,** and **Shana Harrison** in Chile; **Kay Twilley** in Bolivia; **Bob May** in Tonga; and **Irene Mparutsa** and **Jim Gulley** in Cambodia.

The story **John Elmore** told about his call to mission illustrates the way God can use the volunteer experience to lead to a missionary career. John, a building contractor from Alabama, heard a Presbyterian missionary from the Dominican Republic speak at his local United Methodist church. She told about a hospital that was being built there, and about the need for volunteers to help build it. John felt God calling him to go and help, so he sold his house and car, gave away his dog (which he says was the hardest thing he had to do), and went to the Dominican Republic to work on that hospital building.

We met John at a North Alabama Conference Volunteers In Mission Rally at Camp Sumatanga, near Birmingham, after he had been in the Dominican Republic for almost a year. Since he was already working as an individual volunteer but had not heard about our program, we signed him up on the spot.

About a year later, John called our office and said his work in the Dominican Republic was coming to a close and he would like to find another place where he could volunteer. We told him that our friend Stan Moore, a missionary in Chile, was building an agricultural/technical school in the Atacama Desert in northern Chile and could use someone to help receive the volunteer building teams and keep the construction going when teams were not there.

John communicated with Stan and soon began his volunteer work in Chile. Later he decided he wanted to be a career missionary, and we encouraged him to apply for mission service. He was accepted and continues his mission work in Chile.

5. Continuing the Work from Home

Almost without exception, individual volunteers find ways to continue supporting the mission work they have been a part of. The following examples show different ways in which volunteers are able to prolong the mission experience and provide much-needed assistance to the people they have left behind.

Most volunteers are given the opportunity to speak at churches, schools, and civic organizations, and many are able to raise funds to send for special needs that have touched their hearts.

Frank and Mary Hedgcock reported after returning from Bolivia:

> Since April 2001, we have given more than twenty-five slide presentations about our experiences in Bolivia and the work of The Methodist Church there. As a result, the Holy Spirit has moved Rotarians, Presbyterians, and United Methodists to donate over $16,000 to the work of Instituto Americano.
>
> We have purchased more than five hundred books for the library, paid a librarian's salary for two years, and paid for materials and local labor to implement phases one and two of the drainage system. This year we expect to leave sufficient funds with the headmaster to buy the library books on the teachers' "wish list," complete the drainage system with local labor, and install a barbed-wire fence around the campus.

Sharon Romich wrote after returning from her second assignment in Nepal:

> I am planning to organize a fund-raising campaign for the Tansen Mission Hospital. It badly needs renovation and expansion and was denied a USAID grant because it is "not strategic to the American government." So I am going to see what I can do.
>
> I will do this through Louisville and the Presbyterian mission organization so gifts are tax-deductible. I have my first presentation scheduled November 4 at a church. I will show slides at adult Sunday school and then "preach the sermon" during the service that is organized as a praise service by the church women. That will be a first for me. I think I will just tell stories about individual patients and the staff.

Some volunteers are able to help establish markets for goods produced by people in the countries where they served. After their return from Ghana, we were able to visit **Rob and Pam Porter** and their children, **Celia and Drew**, at their home in Sydney, near Vancouver, Canada, and more recently they visited us in Virginia Beach. They brought us a beautiful Ghanaian cloth wall hanging, not from their time in Ghana but from a friend's gift shop in Canada where hand-made items from Ghana are being sold thanks to the Porters' establishing that market for their Ghanaian friends. The mission continues!

Frank and Wini Dressler, after serving in Zimbabwe, assisted a student from Zimbabwe in coming to the United States for his studies. They reported: "Our student completed his undergraduate studies in economics in three and a half years with a GPA of 3.89, took a master's in economics at Iowa State in one year, and is now in the final stages of his PhD at the University of Nevada in Reno."

Morris and Ann Taber found their volunteer work in Zimbabwe so rewarding that they have returned many times to continue the work, and have involved hundreds of people in their campaign to supply the needs of schoolchildren throughout Zimbabwe. A sampling of their reports through the years indicates the success of their continuing efforts:

> For the 1999–2000 school year, 131 more elementary pupils are in school for a year because one person was astounded to learn how far American dollars could go in this poverty-stricken country. One thousand children have a library of roughly eight thousand books. Four bright high school students, whose parents were losing the financial struggle to pay their way, are now getting substantial assistance. A group of secondary teachers returned to their classrooms last week armed with a better understanding of American history and what it means to them and perhaps will be more willing to teach it to their secondary students. Another group will be similarly equipped with texts next year as well. The university library's history section is expanding.

After the dedication of the Hartzell Primary School library, the Tabers thanked the people who had helped by donating books:

> The Hartzell staff prepared and presented an impressive grand opening of the Taber Library. All of you who were a part of that with your books, gifts, and prayers should feel as proud as Ann was that day....

The two-and-a-half-hour program included the entire school, parents, friends, and visiting dignitaries. The recent arrival of a host of books, especially from the Hartland, Michigan, primary schools and Greenhills School in Ann Arbor, meant that the library shelves were impressively stocked....

Classes are coming in on a regular schedule and the free drop-in period sees a steady stream of children. It is a *novelty* in all senses of the word—the excitement of something new, but it is also unique in their experience—this is the first time that they have had access to books, especially ones that have interesting stories, instead of mere exercises. The library is already being spoken of as a model for other schools in the area....

As we had always intended, the library was renamed in honor of Naboth Maramba, now that he has retired as primary school headmaster. The library was his dream, and he built it—right down to the buying of its cement and bricks, and supervising the work. The renaming ceremony was perfect.... His own speech reinforced the accuracy of the tributes paid him. He was still concerned with motivating the children—"The books are no good gathering dust on the shelves. Use them!"

Returning home after their second volunteer assignment in Zimbabwe, the Tabers took on another project—the high school library in Old Mutare:

Hartzell High School's library was in woeful condition and totally unable to meet the needs of its eight hundred students. A grant from the Zimbabwean United Methodist Church provided for the construction of a major addition, but there has been no money for new books for some time.

The problem of books was solved, thanks to the resourcefulness of the Tabers:

As some of you have already heard, we learned of an entire library in a recently closed Catholic High School and decided to think boldly! Again, people from all kinds of places rose to the occasion, and we

179

now have three hundred boxes of books, magazines, and library supplies sitting in our church basement awaiting shipment. A library of six to eight thousand fully processed books is on its way!

Once the books were shipped, Morris wrote:

Getting the library packed up and moved and then assembling everything else that came in while dealing with the brand-new experience of loading and sending eleven hundred cubic feet of "stuff" to Mutare has kept us preoccupied for many, many moons! . . .

Actually, everything went smoothly, and the truck picked up the fully loaded container from the church a few hours ago. But we were never certain how it was going to work out, until it did. We spent most of last week doing final packing, organizing, and labeling the 489 boxes so that we would be able to know what we had, where it was going, and how it needed to be loaded. I moved a lot of boxes—probably a couple of hundred on Saturday alone.

There seemed to be a *lot* of boxes to get inside what Ann felt was a very small container when it arrived on Friday. We were ready for Saturday, but we had no idea how many people would show up to help. Relatively few actually did, but the key person was a fellow from Martin United Methodist Church who loads trucks for a living. Before we seven early birds wore out, eight more arrived at 10:00 a.m., and we were finished by 11:00 a.m. . . .

We never ever dreamed of sending an entire library, to say nothing of the 9 computers, 160 dozen bottles of medicine, 70 boxes of clothes, and sundry other things. But it all seemed to work out. . . . We ended up sending things that came from such faraway places as California, Florida, Maryland, North Carolina, Pennsylvania, and Traverse City. . . . We give thanks to God and to those of you whose efforts made it possible.

After a later visit to Zimbabwe, the Tabers wrote:

A good number of you were a part of the Container Project last year. The impetus for sending the twenty-foot container was the opportunity to ship a complete library from a local closed high school to Hartzell High. The medical supplies have been consumed. The clothes for the orphanage have been put to such good use that recent gifts of that nature have been passed on to other United Methodist orphanages.

The eight additional rebuilt computers are the backbone of a vigorous instruction program at the primary school. One parent is bringing his children eighteen miles each day because of that program! The container has made a big difference in many lives already.

In July 2006, in response to our e-mail telling him our local church in Virginia would be sending several boxes of books for their latest shipment to Zimbabwe, Morris wrote:

> We are finally going to go on a Volunteers In Mission team trip—our first.... We had to close the numbers in early April at thirty (too many!) and we are still at twenty-nine despite everything going on in Zimbabwe. Some others are already talking about us working with another trip next summer. We will have to get through the container and the November trip first!

Summarizing their work on behalf of Zimbabwe from 1999 through 2006, the Tabers wrote in March 2007:

> We have continued the work Ann began in 1999 when she started the Maramba Primary Library at Old Mutare, Zimbabwe. With English the language of instruction and Zimbabwe's official language, *all* schoolchildren must go beyond their mother tongues and learn English. The availability of general-interest books to read has transformed the lives of hundreds of children as their struggle to learn English in order to pass exams became a pleasure and increased their skill.
>
> In September 2006, we sent a third and last container of books and supplies. It included 625 boxes of books. These became the cores for four new primary school libraries.... And that was just the beginning of what was in the container. The VIM network is awesome!

God's Call Continues

We are in awe of the many things that have been accomplished by individual volunteers, and we know that God is still calling people—

young and old and in between—to offer themselves in service to others in the name of Jesus Christ. We are also aware that the volunteers have been able to do great things because of the support they have received from many, many people back home who have prayed for them, taken care of their families, their finances, their businesses, and their property during the volunteers' time of service, and we know God continues to call people to give that kind of support to future volunteers as well.

A devotional in *The Upper Room* dated Wednesday, November 29, 2006, written by James Kwok from the Republic of Singapore, describes the need for volunteers and their supporters in a very eloquent way:

> Jesus said to the apostles, "You will be my witnesses in Jerusalem, in all Judea and Samaria, and to the ends of the earth" (Acts 1:8).
> Like most Chinese, I eat with chopsticks without noticing how I use them. However, chopsticks became an important reminder of Christian service for me after a lunchtime talk a couple of years ago. Brother Fong, one of our missionaries to East Asia who was back in Singapore on furlough, gave the talk. As we prepared to tuck into our boxes of fried rice with our chopsticks, Brother Fong challenged us to eat with only one chopstick instead of a pair. Observing our frustrated attempts, Brother Fong laughed and told us to use our chopsticks the usual way. As we ate he asked us to notice how we use our traditional pair of chopsticks: One stick remains stationary while the other stick moves.
> He said: "Some of us are called to go out into the mission field. We are like the movable stick. Others remain here at home in Singapore to fast and pray for those who travel, to contribute by raising funds and awareness, to extend hospitality to visiting missionaries. These are like the stationary stick." All of us have a part to play according to our God-given gifts.

God continues to call persons to offer themselves for volunteer service, and to call others to support those who go out to serve. The mission statement of The United Methodist Church, updated by the

2008 General Conference, calls upon United Methodists "to make disciples of Jesus Christ for the transformation of the world." We hope that more and more people will respond to God's call so that "the earth will be full of the knowledge of the LORD as the waters cover the sea" (Isaiah 11:9).

9 780687 491094